A Litany of Mary

*OUR LADY OF SORROWS, venerated in Mexico
as La Virgen de los Dolores (see page 165)*

A Litany of Mary

ANN BALL

Our Sunday Visitor Publishing Division
Our Sunday Visitor, Inc.
Huntington, Indiana 46750

Nihil Obstat:
Rev. J. Michael Miller, C.S.B.
Censor Librorum

Imprimatur:
✠ Joseph A. Fiorenza, D.D.
Bishop of Galveston-Houston
May 6, 1987

Our Sunday Visitor Publishing Division
Our Sunday Visitor, Inc.
200 Noll Plaza
Huntington, Indiana 46750

International Standard Book Number: 0-87973-509-0
Library of Congress Catalog Card Number: 87-60142

Cover Design by James E. McIlrath

PRINTED IN THE UNITED STATES OF AMERICA

For my mothers — all three of them:

For the mother who gave me life,
For the mother who taught me how to live,
And for my heavenly Mother, who shows me why I live

Contents

Contents (continued)

Preface: Put Mary in Her Place

MARY, THE MOTHER of Christ, occupies a special place in the hearts of Catholics. It is she to whom many turn for the aid, consolation, and love needed when human needs are not fulfilled and when they need a heavenly Mother. Just as little children sometimes stand in awe of the father of the family and need a mother's hand to hold, many Catholics are led to the Father by the hand of Mary.

Tragically, Mary's role in Catholic theology has often been misunderstood by non-Catholics and Catholics alike. Although all Christians honor her as the Mother of Christ, many are critical of what they perceive as the status accorded her by the Catholic Church. Most of this criticism, we believe, stems from misunderstanding. Unfortunately, Catholics themselves sometimes increase this misunderstanding by their failure to understand the teachings of their own religion and by some of their pious but erroneous customs and actions.

In Roman Catholic theology, God alone is adored as the Almighty, the one true fountain of redemption. God is a triune God — the Father, the Son, and the Holy Spirit. For us, God is honored through His angels and His saints. Mary is a saint and, above that, occupies a special place in the salvation of mankind.

The specific type of love we accord to God and God alone is called *latria*. This is the adoration and love of the one divine Entity. To the saints, we accord a love called *dulia*. We honor, love, respect them, and ask their aid (intercession) because they have been set aside by God through their relationship with Him. For Mary, *hyperdulia* is the type of love we have. Just as with all the saints, we honor her, love and respect her, and ask her intercession. Her love is "hyper," or above, that of the other saints because we believe that God, through His will, gave her a status not enjoyed by anyone else.

Catholics believe that Mary was conceived without the stain of original sin, which was the lot of all of the rest of mankind from the time of the fall from grace of the first man. Nonetheless, this woman conceived without sin was asked by God if she would consent to be the Mother of His Son. Mary could have said no! Just like all of mankind, Mary was given free will. At the Annunciation, Mary gave her consent in her *fiat*: "Let it be done to me according to your word."

Mary lived her life as a good mother to Our Lord. When He was a child and lost in the Temple, she worried about a lost child as any other mother would. At a wedding party, when the hosts were about to be embarrassed by the lack of wine, she told her Son to help.

Each valid Catholic devotion to Mary has a historical basis. Sadly, it is often some of the "trappings" of these devotions which can cause misunderstandings by our non-Catholic Christian brothers and sisters. Let us consider only one — the queenship of Mary. To consider Mary as the queen of all saints, we often refer to her as a queen. A queen is, by birth or action of the king, the most honored woman in a land. At her designation as queen, she is given the symbols of her queenship — a crown and scepter. She is presented with gifts of the best the country has to offer. She reigns over her people. Catholics consider Mary as a queen — a queen of human hearts. This does not mean that they forget the place of the King of Kings — only that they believe He has appointed a queen to assist Him in His reign. However, when Catholics crown images of Our Lady with rich jewels or flowers, and perform pious exercises such as walking to church on their knees, their actions are often mistaken by non-Catholics who may gain the impression that Catholics have, in honoring the Queen, completely forgotten that she reigns only through the action of the King. Does this mean that Catholic devotion to Mary as Queen should be discontinued? No. Only that Catholics must take great care to completely understand their devotions and to be able to explain them to those who truly wish to understand.

Jesus lived fully and completely the human role of a son. When He explained why He had been in the Temple, He still went with His earthly parents and obeyed them. Although He told his mother that it was not time for Him to begin His ministry, He obeyed her wishes and changed water into wine.

At the cross, Mary remained the human mother and shared in the mystery of the Passion by uniting her sorrows to those of her Son. The sorrowful and immaculate heart of Mary bled for her Son and for all of mankind. From the cross, Jesus looked at His Mother and His beloved disciple John. His words to them indicate not only that He wished to provide a surrogate son to care for His mother in her old age, but also that He charged His mother to continue in her motherly ministry, not only to John but to the entire world.

One of the best sermons I ever heard on the devotion to Mary was based on common sense and practical human experience. The minister pointed out that just as we love our own mothers, and are angered and upset if someone does anything to downgrade or hurt her, Christ, in His humanity, must have felt the same way about His own Mother. Just as we humans appreciate it when someone compliments or cares about our mother, Christ, too, is pleased by love extended to His Mother. If, disregarding completely all theological debate, we love Mary on a completely human basis such as this, Christ cannot help but be pleased.

Perhaps because of my own Protestant background, Mary as Mother is one of my favorite titles for Our Lady. I can visualize Mary feeding the infant Jesus, so when I am hungry I find it easy to ask my Mother Mary for spiritual food. As she took joy in watching her Son at work and at play, I, too, take joy in my own children's happiness, and in all of the happinesses of my life. For me it is easy to turn to Mary to tell her to thank her Son for these gifts. Most of all, I can see Our Lady at the foot of the cross, and understand her sorrows at the passion of Our Lord. She knew that He was only on the cross because *He agreed to be there* to save mankind. He was not at fault for any sin of His own. When there is pain in my life, I tell my sorrowful Mother about it. She suffers with me, and helps me dry my tears by reminding me that I was not given promise of an easy or happy earthly life, but that I was promised eternal happiness. My sorrowful Mother reminds me, too, that for every moment of sorrow I feel, I have been blessed with many more days of joy, which I did not earn nor do I deserve. When times are hard, Mother Mary holds her children's hands and helps lead them along the one true Way to her Son, her King, her God. Hers and ours.

Ann Ball
Feast of the Assumption, 1987

12

What Is My Mother's Name?

MY MOTHER has many names and many titles.
Formally, I call her "Mother."

Informally, I call her "Mama."

Usually, though, when I'm calling her, I'm crying, "Help!"
So then I call her. . .

Our Lady of Prompt Succor — meaning "Hurry up and help me. I'm in a real tight jam!"

> or . . .

"Our Lady of Perpetual Help" — meaning that I know she will always help me, no matter how silly my problems are compared to the problems of the rest of the world.

> or . . .

"Our Lady of Grace" — meaning that she has a lot of presents for me, if I am ready to receive them.

> or . . .

"Our Lady of Peace" — meaning that if I would only listen, QUIETLY, I could HEAR so much.

> or . . .

"Our Lady of Guadalupe" — meaning that she has a special message for me, as an American and as Her favored child.

> or . . .

"Our Lady of the Rosary" — meaning that she has given me a help to solve my problems.

> or . . .

"Our Lady of the Miraculous Medal" — meaning that she

has told me a million times how blessed I am to have a Mother who will do so much for me in so many ways.

or . . .

"Our Lady Thrice Admirable" — meaning that she will remind me that she has more than one way of saying she loves me, and that we have a covenant, or a promise of love to each other.

or . . .

"Our Lady of the Atocha" — meaning that she wants to remind me that I only ask her for things because she is the Mother of the "Child Who Moves Hearts" (*Santo Niño Mueve Corazónes*). She reminds me that, although I honor her, I am always to direct my love to her divine Son.

or . . .

"Our Lady of Love" — meaning that, in the end, She will show me what is most important in my life to help me arrive at the pot of gold at the end of the rainbow!

This is what I call my Mother.

This is a Litany of Mary.

'My Name Is Mary'

"Oh, how I praise the Lord. How I rejoice in God my Savior! For he took notice of his lowly servant girl, and now generation after generation forever shall call me blest of God. For he, the mighty Holy One, has done great things to me." (Lk 1:46-49, *Living Bible Trans.*)

MY NAME IS Mary. After my Son, Jesus Christ, lived as man on earth, generation after generation indeed has called me favored by God. In keeping with my commitment to the will of God, I continue to assist in His plan for the salvation of all mankind. In addition to calling me blessed, generation after generation has called on me for help. Often I have been God's messenger, bringing tidings of faith and hope, carrying communications requesting mankind to remember God's mercy and His justice. Many times I have wept and pleaded with my children to turn away from their unruly and sinful ways, and to return to face the brightness of God's countenance. From the joy of Christmas to the grief of Good Friday, I have been privileged to be the faithful handmaid of the Lord.

I am known by many titles, called on by many names, in every nation of the earth. No matter what my title, no matter by which name I am called, my name is Mary.

15

*VIRGIN EPISKEPSIS, fresco in the Church
of St. Clement, Ohrid, Yugoslavia (Ancora)*

Part I:
A Litany of Mary

THROUGH THE ages, Mary, the Mother of God, has been given hundreds of titles. Some of her titles are biblical; some are titles of love and respect. Most titles refer to a geographical location. In her apparitions (or appearances) she has often given her titles or names which recall the message she has come to earth to bring. Following are some principal titles and their stories.

OUR LADY OF THE
ATOCHA — the statue
at Fresnillo, Zacatecas,
Mexico, also venerated
in the United States

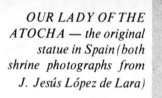

OUR LADY OF THE
ATOCHA — the original
statue in Spain (both
shrine photographs from
J. Jesús López de Lara)

Our Lady of the Atocha

W HEREVER HISPANIC Catholics live, Our Lady of the Atocha and her beloved Santo Niño de Atocha are honored and loved. Images of the Lady and her little Boy, with His floppy, feathered hat, occupy a special place in Spanish homes, places of business, and hearts. Many who honor Our Lady and her Son under this title do not know the story behind the devotion. They only know what is important to them — their prayers are answered. Those of Mexican or Hispanic heritage have a saying about Him, "*Santo Niño mueve corazónes*" — "The Holy Child moves hearts."

Tradition says devotion to Our Lady of Atocha originated in Antioch, and that St. Luke the Evangelist was the sculptor of the first Mother-and-Child image. Thus, Atocha could be a corruption of Antiochia. The devotion spread rapidly, and by 1162 it had come to Spain. The statue was in Toledo in the Church of St. Leocadia. In 1523, Charles V of Spain paid for an enormous temple and placed the statue under the care of the Dominicans. The image of the Divine Child was detachable, and devout families would borrow the image of the infant when a woman was about to give birth to her child.

The story of the miraculous nature of the statue begins in Spain during the dark years of the Moorish invaders. The Spanish were persecuted for their faith. In Atocha, a suburb

19

of Madrid, many of the Spanish men were thrown into Moorish dungeons. As the Moors did not feed their prisoners, food was taken to them by their families. During one persecution, an order went out from the caliph in Atocha that no one except children twelve years old and younger would be permitted to bring food to the prisoners. Those with young children would manage to keep their relatives alive, but what of the others?

The women of the town went to the parish church where there was a statue of Our Lady of Atocha holding the baby Jesus which had been venerated for many years. They begged Our Lady to help them find a way to feed their husbands, sons, and brothers. Soon the children came home from the prison with a strange story. Those prisoners who had no young children to feed them were being visited and fed by a young boy. None of the children knew who he was, but the little water gourd he carried was never empty, and there was always plenty of bread in his basket to feed all of the hapless prisoners without children to bring them their food. He always came at night, slipping past the sleeping guards, or smiling politely at those who were alert. Those who had asked the Virgin of Atocha for a miracle began to suspect the identity of the little boy. As if in confirmation of the miracle they had prayed for, the shoes on the statue of the child Jesus were worn down. When they replaced the shoes with new ones, these, too, were worn out.

After Ferdinand and Isabella drove the Moors from Spain in 1492, the people continued to invoke the aid of Our Lady and her Holy Child. They especially asked help for those in jail or "imprisoned" in the mines.

When the Spaniards came to the New World, they brought along the devotions of their native regions. Those from Madrid naturally brought their devotion to Our Lady and her miracle-working pilgrim Infant. In 1540, silver mines were found in Mexico, and mineworkers migrated here. In Plateros, a tiny village near the mines of Fresnillo, a church was built in honor of El Niño de Santa Maria de Atocha. Here the Holy Child continued His miracle-working for those who appealed to him, through His mother, for help. Soon the shrine became a major place of pilgrimage. The original statue in Plateros shrine was donated by a rich mine owner. It was made as a duplicate of the one in Spain. It, too, had a removable infant which could be borrowed. The infant at one time was lost, and when a replacement was carved to size to be affixed to the original statue, the new babe had Indian features. Those whose prayers were answered left *retablos* in thanksgiving. These are pictures painted on wood or on tin in which folk artists show the story of a miracle. There are few words, but the pictures tell the story of the miracles. There are *retablos* here dating from the 1500s to our own times. In Mexico, a land of many churches, only the shrine of Our Lady of Guadalupe has more of these thanksgiving plaques. Through a century of revolution, Mexico has provided many prisoners for the Holy Child to aid. Annually, other miraculous cures and escapes are reported here.

The original statue of Our Lady of the Atocha in the shrine holds the Holy Child in her left arm. Over the years, the manner of portraying the Holy Child and His Mother changed slightly, according to the changes in custom and fashions. They are seen today as they have been since the eighteenth century. The child Jesus wears a velvet suit with a wide lace collar and frilled cuffs. He has a broad hat with feathers. His shoes are buckled. In Mexico, the shoes are usually made of silver or gold. He carries a basket of bread and a staff from which hangs his water gourd. The cockleshell on His short cape derives from His Spanish origin. It is a Spanish symbol denoting that He is a pilgrim.

In the 1800s, a man from New Mexico made a pilgrimage to Fresnillo and took back with him a small statue of the Holy Child. This statue was enshrined in Chimayo, near Santa Fe. Here the devotion grew as in Mexico.

Some of the first American troops to see action in World War II were from the New Mexico National Guard. They fought bravely on Corregidor, with its underground tunnels and defenses. The Catholics remembered that the Santo Niño de Atocha had long been considered a patron of all who were trapped or imprisoned. Many of them made a vow that if they survived the war, they would make a pilgrimage from Santa Fe to Chimayo in thanksgiving. At the end of the war, two thousand pilgrims, veterans of Corregidor, the Bataan death march, and Japanese prison camps, together with their families, walked the long and rough road from Santa Fe to Chimayo. Some walked barefoot to the little adobe shrine.

The prayers and novenas to the miracle-working little child Jesus all begin with prayers to Our Lady of the Atocha. As Jesus is shown as a small child, first His clients have to ask His mother's permission for Him to go to their aid. As in all true Marian devotions, the holy Virgin is begged for her intercession with her Son.

Beloved Virgin Mary of Atocha, through your intercession obtain for me from your divine Child my freedom from my self-made prisons of sin. I beg you to ask your pilgrim Son to deliver me from all the evils of the day, and to lead me on my pilgrimage through life to my heavenly home.

22

Our Lady of the Atonement

A T THE LAST SUPPER, Our Lord prayed "That all may be one." At the foot of the cross, Mary shared in Christ's redeeming action for all mankind. The title of Our Lady of the Atonement is a title of unity. One of the many unusual facts about this title is that devotion to Mary under this name began outside of the Catholic Church.

The Rosary League of Our Lady of the Atonement was formed in 1901 with the purpose "to pray and work for the restoration of Mary's Dowry, England, to our Virgin Queen, the Holy Mother of God." Later, the object of the league became more extensive and included not only the conversion of England but that of the entire world. The league was formed by Father Paul (Lewis Thomas) Wattson and Mother Lurana (Mary Francis) White, members of the Anglican communion until they, with fifteen others, were received into the Catholic Church in 1909. The little community grew and is now known as the Society of the Atonement, or the Franciscan friars and sisters of Graymoor. In 1919, Pope Benedict XV gave his approval and apostolic recognition to the title of Our Lady of the Atonement.

In the beautiful representation of Mary under this title, she wears a red mantle, symbolizing the Precious Blood, of which she was the immaculate source and by which she was made immaculate. It was by the shedding of this most precious blood that the redemption of the world was accom-

23

OUR LADY OF THE ATONEMENT, painting by Mother Nealis
(Franciscans of the Atonement, Graymoor, Garrison, N.Y.)

plished. She wears a blue inner tunic, and she holds the infant Jesus in her arms. The child Jesus is depicted holding a cross, the symbol of His suffering and glory.

The concept of Our Lady of the Atonement includes two parts. First, it emphasizes Mary's role as co-redemptrix in the mystery of the cross. Secondly, it points to Mary's role in effecting the unity or "At-one-ment" of men with God. Mary cooperated with Christ as no other creature did in His work of reconciling man with God. In honoring Mary with this title, we remember her with gratitude and love for the great gift of her Son to us, just as Christ in His death on the cross, gave Mary to us to be our Mother . . . "Behold your Mother."

Mary is Our Lady of Unity, Our Lady of the At-one-ment. Even those who are separated from the Church still have a claim upon her charity, and she longs to unite them to her divine Son. Just as the father's heart went out to His prodigal son in love and forgiveness, Mary's Immaculate Heart reaches out to her children who have wandered from the Father. Father Wattson, in speaking of Mary's longing for all mankind to come to her Son, said, "She will not be satisfied until all the Children of Eve dwelling upon the face of the earth in all parts of the world have been born again into the Kingdom of Heaven and numbered among the elect Children of the Atonement." Christian-unity work always lends itself to a special emphasis on Mary's role. Our Lady is the Refuge of Sinners, the Help of Christians, the Mother of Mercy, and the Mother of Perpetual Help. More than any other being save God Himself, she desires men to be saved and to come to her Son.

Even those who do not call on her receive love and grace from Mary's Immaculate Heart. Although the atonement emphasizes Mary's sorrow, it also calls to mind her joy when a soul is saved. In the words of Our Lord, "Your sorrows are for a little while; your joys are eternal."

Pope John Paul II said, "The Week of Prayer for Christian Unity is ever more harmoniously celebrated among Catholics, Orthodox, and Protestants. It is now spread throughout the world." By honoring Mary with the title Our Lady of Atonement, we call to mind her wish that our prayers will be unceasing for the reunion of all God's sheep under one Shepherd.

Our Lady of the Atonement, help me to win souls both by my prayers and by my actions. Let me assist the Divine Shepherd in gathering all of His lost sheep into the fold.

Our Lady of Banneux:
The Virgin of the Poor

WHERE CAN Julien be?" Anxiously, eleven-year-old Mariette Beco was waiting the return of her younger brother. Night was falling, and Julien should long since have returned. Mariette, the oldest of the seven Beco children, stopped rocking the baby and went to peer out a front window to see if she could catch a glimpse of her brother. It was Sunday night, January 15, 1933.

There in the garden was the luminous figure of a young woman. At first, Mariette thought that it was a reflection from the oil lamp. After moving the lamp to another position, she looked again. The figure was still there. The woman was very beautiful, about five feet tall. She was dressed in a white gown with a blue sash. A rosary hung from her right hand. Only her right foot was visible, and it was adorned with a golden rose. Her head was inclined a little to the left, and she appeared to be smiling at Mariette.

Mariette called to her mother, "There's a woman in the garden!" Mrs. Beco accepted this remark with skepticism until Mariette insisted she come and look for herself. Looking out the window, she could only discern a white shape. Somewhat frightened, she told Mariette it might be a witch. She ordered her daughter to shut the curtain and come away.

27

Not long before, Mariette had found a set of rosary beads lying in the road. She got them and said a few decades. As she watched, the lips of the lady moved, but Mariette could hear nothing. Then the lady beckoned to Mariette. As Mariette made to go outside, her mother forbade it. When Mariette returned to the window, the lady had disappeared.

When young Julien came home, the family went to bed. The elder Julien and her mother had told Mariette to forget the strange sight.

The next morning, Mariette went over in detail with her father what had happened. Mr. Beco, a badly lapsed Catholic, told her that the story was nonsense. Nonetheless, he later asked his wife to show him where in he garden she had seen the shadowy figure. When he asked Mariette where she had seen the lady, she pointed to the exact same spot. That night, Mr. Beco experimented with the lamp, but could not re-create any illusion.

On the Monday after this apparition, Mariette went to school for the first time in two months. She confided the strange tale to her friend Josephine Léonard, whose first reaction was disbelief. Seeing how upset Mariette was at not being believed, Josephine suggested the girls go and tell the parish priest, Father Louis Jamin. Father Jamin, thinking the girl must have heard of the recent apparition in Beauraing, advised her not to speak of seeing the Blessed Mother.

That night and the next, Mariette looked through the window to see if she could again see the beautiful lady. Although she saw nothing, she was convinced that she had seen Our Lady, and there was a great change in her behavior. She began to study her catechism, and the next day she attended Mass and said her prayers.

*OUR LADY OF BANNEUX: Virgin of the Poor,
sculpture by Dupont for the shrine at Banneux
(St. Meinrad Press, St. Meinrad Archabbey, Ind.)*

Wednesday night, just before seven, Mariette went outside. Her father followed her and found her kneeling before the spot where she said she had seen the lady three days before. She was saying her Rosary.

Suddenly Mariette stretched out her arms. She could see the figure of her lady floating toward her through the pines. The figure came to a halt about a yard and a half in front of Mariette. Her feet didn't touch the ground, but rested on a grayish cloud about a foot off the ground. The lady appeared the same, except this time Mariette noticed that she had a halo. Mariette continued to pray. Her father jumped on his bicycle and went to tell the priest what was happening. The priest was not in, so he persuaded a neighbor and his son to come back with him. As they arrived, Mariette walked out of the garden and approached them on the road. When they asked where she was going, Mariette simply said, "She is calling me."

Twice Mariette dropped to her knees on the ground. Then she continued walking. Abruptly she turned right and knelt at the brink of a small stream. The lady stood on the other bank and spoke for the first time, telling Mariette to put her hands in the water. Mariette obeyed. Then the lady told Mariette that the spring was reserved for her, and said "*Au revoir*" (good-bye for the present). Although only Mariette could hear the words, she repeated them aloud. The lady then slowly withdrew into the sky, growing smaller and smaller until she disappeared.

Later that evening Father Jamin returned home and was told what had happened. In company with a Benedictine monk and a friend, he went to the Beco household and had a long conversation with Mr. Beco. Mariette was sleeping, and they did not disturb her. When the priest asked Mr. Beco if he believed Mariette had seen the Virgin, he answered yes, and he asked to come to confession the next day.

The following evening, Mariette experienced a third apparition. Again she returned to the spring at the insistance of the figure. Here she asked the apparition about her statement that the spring was reserved for her. The smiling lady said, "For all the nations . . . for the sick . . . I come to relieve the sick." Following the advice of the priest's Benedictine friend, Mariette asked the lady, "Who are you, Madame?" The lady said to her, "I am the Virgin of the Poor."

In all, there were eight appearances. During the fourth apparition, Mariette asked if the Lady wanted anything and was told she would like a little chapel. In the other apparitions, the message was given, "I come to relieve suffering." Asked for a sign, the lady replied, "Have faith in me . . . I shall trust you . . . Pray earnestly."

At the sixth appearance, Mariette was entrusted with a secret which she has never revealed.

At the final apparition, the Virgin said, "I am the Mother of the Savior, Mother of God. Pray hard." Then she spoke the parting word, "*Adieu*," and imposed a blessing on Mariette. Mariette fainted, and did not see Our Lady's departure. She knew, however, that this would be her final sight of the beautiful lady from the choice of the word "*adieu*" (good-bye) instead of the previously used "*au revoir*."

For several years, Mariette was subject to every kind of test. She was examined by panels of doctors and psychiatrists. None could find any trace of hysteria or untruth.

As with any reported apparitions, those at Banneux were investigated thoroughly. A number of miraculous medical cures were claimed through the prayers and the use of the water at Banneux. Although not accepted as proofs, these are accepted as presumptions in favor of the apparitions. Within a year of the apparitions, the bishop approved the establishment of the worldwide "International Union of Prayers." Today, this group has more than two million members throughout the world, all pledged to say a prayer of their own choice daily in union with those sent up from Banneux for the poor, the suffering, and for peace on earth. In 1942, as a result of the unanimous verdict of the Ecclesiastical Commission, supported by rescripts of approval from the Holy See, the bishop authorized by pastoral letter the cult of Our Lady of Banneux, Our Lady of the Poor. This approval was renewed and confirmed in 1947, and again in 1949.

The message of Our Lady at Banneux, while given through a single child, is a message for all her children. "I come to relieve suffering." As Our Lady drew Mariette to the water of a healing spring, she draws us all to the living water of Christ Jesus. By declaring herself the Virgin of the Poor, she reminds us of her love and concern for all of mankind.

Our Lady of Banneux, Blessed Virgin of the Poor, look with favor on us, your poor, suffering children. Hear our prayers, and draw us daily to the Living Water.

Our Lady of Częstochowa:
'The Black Madonna'

BEHIND THE Iron Curtain, in the city of Częstochowa, Poland, is a church which contains a painting of Our Lady that is venerated by many as an actual portrait of the Madonna, painted during her lifetime by St. Luke the Evangelist on the top surface of a cypress-wood table. Although the original painting is locked in by political iron, her image has escaped throughout the world and is honored worldwide by both Polish nationals and all those who love the freedom that God has given to each soul.

An ancient legend tells how the painting was brought to Poland. Nothing is known of the first years of the picture's history. In 326, when St. Helena went to Jerusalem to search for the true cross, she also found the picture of Our Lady. She gave the picture to her son, Constantine, who had a shrine built for it in Constantinople. There it was credited with saving the city from attacking Saracens when it was displayed from the city's walls during the battle.

Years later the Emperor Charlemagne visited Constantinople, and when he was offered his choice of any of the treasures in the city, he chose only the portrait of Our Lady. Charlemagne presented the painting to Prince Leo of Ruthenia.

For hundreds of years, the picture remained at the royal

OUR LADY OF CZĘSTOCHOWA, "The Black Madonna," painting at shrine, Jasna Gora, Poland

palace. Then enemy troops invaded the country. Urgently the king prayed to Our Lady to aid his tiny army. Through the intercession of Our Lady, a heavy darkness fell on the enemy, and in the confusion they began destroying their own troops. Later, Prince Ladislaus of Opola had a dream in which the Blessed Mother requested him to take her picture to the Mount of Light (*Jasna Gora*) in Poland. He brought the picture at once and entrusted it to a group of Pauline Fathers.

The monks built a shrine for the painting at Częstochowa, and countless miraculous events occurred there. Soon it became the most famous shrine in Poland.

Once, bandits attempted to steal the miraculous painting. When they attempted to carry away the picture, the wagon would not move. One of the bandits became infuriated and threw the painting on the ground. Grabbing his sword, he slashed away at the picture. As he raised his weapon to slash again, he fell dead. The other bandits ran in terror, and the painting was returned to its place of honor.

Either fires or centuries of votive candles have darkened the image, whence the popular title "Black Madonna."

In 1655, enemy troops invaded Poland, and all of the country was conquered except the shrine of the Black Madonna. A small group of monks and soldiers determined to defend the shrine, even at the cost of death. For forty days the brave little band staved off the invading army, and at last the invaders retreated. This victory gave the Polish people new courage, and they drove the enemy out of the country.

The King of Poland placed the country under the protection of the Blessed Mother, and named Our Lady of Częstochowa the queen of the crown of Poland.

Today, Poland is a communist-controlled country. The

35

Black Madonna remains, however, the queen of Polish Catholics.

Our Lady of Częchowa, help me always to remember my oppressed and persecuted brothers, and to follow your lead in taking action to release them from their captors, whether these be sin, poverty, prejudice, or political ideologies.

Our Lady of Fátima:
Pilgrim of Peace

FROM DIOCESE to diocese, a beautiful statue of the Immaculate Heart of Mary travels to visit her people. The statue, breathtaking in its beauty, is a symbol of the more beautiful heart of the Mother of Peace. She brings with her the ageless message that Christ is our Redeemer, that He is Love and Mercy, and the Giver of every grace. The pilgrim mother visits to remind her children that they offend God by their sin and to request them to offer reparation for their sins and those of others. If her message is heeded, she promises an era of peace for mankind. Her Immaculate Heart will triumph.

The pilgrim statue serves as a reminder of the message Mary herself brought through three young shepherd children at Fátima, Portugal. She began her message on May 13, 1917, when she appeared at the Cova da Iria. After promising to take them to heaven, she asked the children if they were willing to offer themselves to God as an act of reparation for the sins by which He was being offended and in supplication for the conversion of sinners.

The children willingly offered themselves.

The youngsters' story was received by their families, and later by ecclesiastical and civil authorities, with skeptical disbelief.

OUR LADY OF FATIMA: "Pilgrim Virgin" Statue
making parish visitations throughout the world

According to the children, the vision had been preceded by several visits of an angel who had taught them certain prayers. On May 13, as they tended their sheep, a strong wind arose, and they were frightened by a flash of lightning. A brilliant white light moved toward them, stopping at last on top of a small oak tree. Within the light, they saw a beautiful Lady, her hands closed in prayer. She had rosary beads dangling from her fingers. She requested the children to make sacrifices, to say the Rosary for peace, and she promised to return on the thirteenth of each month until the following October. Later requests reiterated her wish for the Rosary to be said for peace, for the consecration of Russia to her Immaculate Heart, and for Communion on the first Saturday of each month.

During the summer months, others began to accompany the children. Although only the children could see the vision, it seemed obvious to onlookers that they were seeing something. The anticlerical authorities arrested the children and threatened them in order to make them recant, but the children steadfastly held to their story of the visions.

The Lady had promised a great miracle for October 13, and it is estimated that there were about seventy thousand people gathered at the Cova da Iria on that date. A heavy rain had fallen all morning, and the entire area was a sea of mud. At the appointed time, in the midst of thunder and lightning, a dazzling cloud of light appeared. Our Lady appeared and requested that a chapel be built there to honor her. Then she showed three scenes to the children. She showed them the Holy Family first, then Our Lord bearing the cross with the Mother of Sorrows beside him, and finally Our Lady was shown crowned as the Queen of Heaven, holding the Divine Child on her knees and extending the Carmelite scapular to the crowd.

Suddenly, Lucy cried, "Look at the sun!" The rain abruptly stopped and the sun seemed to spin about on its axis, and then it seemed to descend toward the earth. Clouds, trees, people and other objects appeared to change colors constantly. As the sun appeared to descend, many fell to their knees while others ran in fright. Suddenly the downward course of the sun stopped, and it resumed its normal position. Those present discovered that their clothes were completely dry. Thousands of eyewitnesses have testified to the miraculous events of that day.

True to a prediction of Our Lady, both Francisco and Jacinta died within two years after the apparitions. Lucy attended a boarding school and became a lay sister for the Sisters of St. Dorothy. Nearly thirty years after the apparitions, Lucy visited Fatima again briefly before becoming a cloistered Carmelite.

A wealthy Portuguese man named Gilberto went to Fatima on May 13, 1920, but his pilgrimage plans did not include prayers. Filled with bitterness for reasons known only to himself, he went with the intention of throwing bombs at the pilgrims he would find there. Heaven intervened, and Gilberto returned home converted.

On Thanksgiving, for the peace he now felt, he hired the most widely known sculptor in Portugal, José Thedim, to carve a statue resembling the vision of Our Lady the three children had seen. This statue was crowned by a papal legate in 1946, and given the title of "Queen of the World." The statue is kept in the chapel at the Cova da Iria and is carried in procession on the thirteenth of each month from May to October.

A copy of the original statue was carved by the same sculptor by request of the first Bishop of Fatima. During a youth congress in 1947, a resolution was passed to have a statue carried throughout Europe and into Russia. Lucy suggested that the bishop give his statue for this purpose and that it be known as the "Pilgrim Virgin." In 1947, a second Pilgrim Virgin statue was blessed for the Americas. Another statue, blessed at the same time, was secretly taken into Russia in 1950. In 1967, more statues were blessed to be presented to individual countries around the world.

Today, the Pilgrim Virgin statues travel around the world, going from diocese to diocese, to bring the message of Fatima to all God's children. Information about the statues in the United States may be obtained from the Blue Army, P.O. Box 976, Washington, N.J. 07882.

Immaculate Heart of Mary, help me to realize how much my smallest sin offends and hurts my God. Remind me to do penance for my own sins, and for those of others, that we may speedily see peace in this world and everlasting peace after our days on earth.

Our Lady of Guadalupe

ALTHOUGH SHE is the patroness of all the Americas, many Americans do not know the story of Our Lady of Guadalupe. Some know *how* she came — to the Indian Juan Diego — but few know *why* she came.

In the beginning of the sixteenth century in Mexico, an idolatrous worship of Quetzalcoatl and other gods flourished. Although Mexico had been conquered for Spain by Cortez, the Indians still held to their ancient religion, which emphasized human sacrifice.

In the Aztec nation alone, twenty thousand human lives were sacrificed annually to their gods. One particularly popular form of sacrifice was to cut the heart out of a still-living human victim.

One of the primary purposes of Mary's visitation, then, was to stamp out the religion of the stone serpent. That this purpose was fulfilled is shown by the fact that within seven years, eight million Indians had come voluntarily to the Franciscans and other missionaries and requested instructions and baptism. This fact is even more amazing when you consider that the Indians in their pagan religion had many wives, but upon becoming Christians were obliged to choose only one and be married according to the rites of the Church.

Our Lady appeared to Juan Diego, a Christian convert, on the hill of Tepayac on December 9, 1531. She requested

OUR LADY OF GUADALUPE: miraculous image on tilma at the rebuilt basilica shrine in Mexico City, Mexico

that he go to the Bishop of Mexico, in Mexico City, and ask that a church be built on the spot. The hill held special significance in the pagan religion of the Indians. At first the bishop refused the appeal, thinking that Juan was merely imagining things. The next day, Our Lady appeared again and repeated her request. This time, Juan was so sincere in his petition that the bishop was more inclined to listen and told Juan to ask the lady for some sort of a sign as proof of the apparition. At a third meeting, Juan mentioned the bishop's request, and the lady promised to give the sign the following morning. On the morning of December 12, Juan awoke to discover that his aged uncle was very ill, and he left hurriedly to bring a priest from the city to administer the last rites. As he neared the hill, he remembered the request of the lady and, thinking that she would delay him, he hurried around the side of the bottom of the hill to avoid her. There she was, however, and when she asked him where he was going, he explained about his sick relative.

Our Lady assured Juan that his uncle would recover, and then sent him to the top of the hill to fetch some flowers for her. Juan knew that nothing grew there except some cactus, so he was greatly surprised to find many flowers in bloom. He picked a large bouquet, and so as not to drop them, he put them in his *tilma*, a cloak woven of vegetable fiber.

When Juan reached the lady again, she tied the ends of the tilma at his neck and charged him not to show the flowers to anyone until he was in the presence of the bishop.

On reaching the bishops' palace again, and after a lengthy wait, Juan was at last admitted to the bishop's presence. Only then did he unfold his tilma. Castilian roses cascaded to the floor. Immediately, all those in the room fell to their knees. Did the sight of out-of-season, foreign flowers inspire this reaction? No. Instead, it was the sight of the beautiful image of the Blessed Virgin, imprinted on the tilma just as she had appeared on the hill.

Juan rushed home to tell his uncle, but his uncle was coming to meet him with the news that he, too, had seen the beautiful lady. She had spoken in his native language, and told him that the image was to be known by the name of the "Entirely Perfect Virgin, Holy Mary," and that the image would be the means to crush or stamp out the religion of the stone serpent.

Juan and his uncle spoke to the Spanish bishop through the use of interpreters, and when they were telling about Mary's words to Juan's uncle, or so most modern scholars believe, the words they spoke were not translated correctly. To the Spanish ears of the translator, their words seemed to say that the image was to be known by the name "Virgin of Guadalupe," which was the name of a popular shrine in Spain dedicated to the Virgin.

Is the image really miraculous, or only a painting? It has been studied from time to time by various experts from all fields, and all are in agreement that no artistic process currently known on earth was used to make the picture.

One artist who made a detailed examination of the image came to these conclusions: 1. He could find no brush marks. 2. The cloth had never been prepared for painting. 3. The cloth was authentically a product of that time. 4. No known painting process was used. 5. None of the colors actually penetrated into the threads of the tilma.

The same artist further concluded that the gold on the picture is a precious gold powder which is not held on by any fixative or glue. The fine black lines which outline the picture were drawn on by human hands at a later date, as was a crown which was not originally on the image. It is interesting to note that the crown, although of real gold, has tarnished and almost disappeared, whereas the other gold on the image is still in good condition.

The image is sixty-six inches by forty-one inches, and the figure is four feet eight inches tall. This apparently makes the image life-size. This artist marvels that the colors have stayed fresh, although most old paintings approximately four hundred and fifty years of age have become dull and dark. It is doubly amazing when you consider that for the first one hundred sixteen years the tilma was not covered with glass but exposed to the smoke of millions of candles burned at the feet of the image.

The image is constantly being studied. After a shrine visitor noticed something in the eyes of the image, a commission which had as members several distinguished optometrists as well as artists studied the eyes of the image. A reflection of a man, probably Juan Diego, has been found imprinted on the eye of the Virgin.

Twenty popes have issued decrees concerning the image. Each year's investigations are made with increasingly accurate and scientific equipment. To date, there has been nothing found to indicate that the picture could have been made by human hands.

Is this image a true picture of the Virgin Mary? The Bible does not describe the Virgin, and the only two sources which many scholars rely on in the matter of description are a painting which was discovered in the catacombs in 1852 and the descriptions given by people who claim to have seen a vision of Blessed Mother. In particular, the descriptions given by a German peasant girl, Anne Catherine Emmerich, are quite detailed. Comparisons of Anne's description and the painting from the catacombs with the image of Guadalupe yield startling similarities. Unlike the pictures of

Our Lady of Lourdes, Fatima, and other paintings made by human hands from verbal descriptions of those who saw Our Lady, the image of Guadalupe, as far as is known, was made by some process above the laws of nature. It is, therefore, the most accurate representation of Mary extant.

Millions of pilgrims come to the shrine each year. Unfortunately, not everyone loves and venerates Our Lady, and in 1921, during the revolution and the persecution of Catholics in Mexico, a stick of dynamite hidden in a bouquet of flowers was placed on the altar to destroy the image. It exploded, causing a great deal of damage. It broke all of the windows in the church, tore out marble blocks from the altar, and knocked a heavy bronze crucifix standing under the image to the floor, leaving it bent and twisted. Nothing, however, happened to the image. The glass which covers it was not even cracked. The preservation of the image in this case is miraculous in itself.

In 1976, work on a new basilica was completed and the shrine rededicated. Study and research on the image continues, and annually thousands flock to the site to pay homage to Mary under the title Our Lady of Guadalupe.

Our Lady of Guadalupe, when the false gods of money, pride, and self-will demand my attention, draw me back to the One True God.

47

OUR LADY HELP OF CHRISTIANS painting by Lorenzone

Detail from Tommaso Lorenzone painting at St. John Bosco's basilica in honor of Our Lady Help of Christians in Turin, Italy

Our Lady Help of Christians:
'Maria, Hilf!' (Mary, Help!)

MARIAN DEVOTION gradually unfolded throughout the centuries, and the theory of Mary as helper gradually emerged into the explicit title of Help of Christians.

Over a thousand Byzantine texts of early times refer to Mary as "Empress Helper." An inscription found among the ruins of fifth-century African basilicas reads, "Holy Mary, help us." By the tenth century, the Greek liturgy had a special patronage of Mary asking for her help as God gave to Mary "the office of protecting the Christian people." The title "Mary Help of Christians" has been found in the Litanies of Loreto from the sixteenth century.

Victories attributed to the intercession of Our Lady at the Battle of Lepanto in 1571 and again at the Battle of Vienna in 1683 popularized the title Help of Christians. This title became historically intertwined with the titles Our Lady of Victory and Our Lady of the Rosary.

A picture of Our Lady painted in the mid 1500s was enshrined in a public shrine built in 1624 in honor of Mary Help of Christians in Passau, Bavaria. Pilgrims to this shrine prayed the short prayer, *"Maria, hilf."* In 1627, Pope Urban VIII approved a confraternity of Mary Help of Christians of Passau. In 1684, after the decisive victory against the Muslims at Vienna, a confraternity in honor of Mary Help of Christians was set up in Munich by a bull of Pope Innocent XI.

In the early 1800s, Napoleon Bonaparte virtually imprisoned Pope Pius VII. From his isolation, the Pope organized an intense rosary campaign of prayer to Mary Help of Christians. As a sign of gratitude for Mary's help, on the abdication of Napoleon and the release of the Pope, Pius VII instituted the feast of Our Lady Help of Christians to be celebrated on May 24 of every year. Again, spiritual victory, the Rosary, and the title Mary Help of Christians are intertwined.

St. John Bosco was born one month before the institution of the feast of Mary Help of Christians. It was to be one of his particular hallmarks in life to be a great apostle of Our Lady under this title. Throughout his life, Don Bosco had a deep personal devotion to Mary. The title Help of Christians seemed to his astute social conscience to be a title most needed in his day. He relied on her for temporal and spiritual aid. He began work on a church in honor of Our Lady Help of Christians at a time when many thought him insane, for he did not have the resources to begin such a project, much less complete it. Time after time he asked Our Lady's aid, and the basilica stands as a monument to faith in her for whom it is named. More important than reliance on her for temporal aid, Don Bosco considered devotion to Mary important in securing help in leading a Christian life. One of the most important legacies Don Bosco left to the members of his Salesian family was the devotion to Our Lady Help of Christians. To promote devotion to the Blessed Sacrament and to Our Lady, he founded the Archconfraternity of Mary Help of Christians. He founded the Salesian Sisters to carry on for girls the work the Salesian Fathers and Brothers were doing for boys, and gave them the name Daughters of Mary Help of Christians. A special work he initiated for vocations was called the Work of Mary Help of Christians, and a group of his young men destined for the foreign missions came to be called Sons of Mary Help of Christians. The successors of St. John Bosco have continued to promote the devotion to Mary Help of Christians and, after Vatican Council II, called for world-wide renewal of devotion to Mary.

Mary, Help of Christians, come to my aid. Assist me in my temporal needs, and help me to live in such a manner that I may obtain the promise of everlasting life.

Our Lady of La Salette

THE BEAUTIFUL LADY was crying. She was weeping as if her heart was breaking — and all because of her child . . . and all of the children of the world.

The young man was dying. Poor, unhappy, and unstable, he drew up his testament. "In the name of the Father and of the Son and of the Holy Spirit, Amen. I believe in all that the holy, apostolic, Roman Church teaches, in everything defined by our Holy Father, the Pope, the august and infallible Pius IX. I firmly believe, even were it to cost the shedding of my blood, in the renowned apparition of the Blessed Virgin on the holy mountain of La Salette, September 19, 1846, the apparition to which I have testified in words, in writings, and in suffering. After my death let no one assert that he has heard me make any retraction concerning the great event of La Salette, for in lying to the world he would be lying in his own breast. With these sentiments, I give my heart to Our Lady of La Salette."

The body of Maximin Giraud was buried in the place of his birth. His heart, according to his specific and earnest wish, was placed in the basilica on the mountain dedicated to the sad and beautiful lady who chose him to bring a message to the world. A failure by worldly standards, he remained true to the one who had chosen him.

The old woman in a black dress and an outdated bonnet was not in her usual place before the altar. As she was such a faithful and familiar figure in the church, some of the people went to the house where she boarded to see if she was all right. When loud knocks at her locked door brought no response, the door was forced. There, dressed for her walk to Mass, Melanie Mathieu lay dead. She who had been given, for a brief time, a great charisma, died alone — a stubborn and seemingly forsaken, prideful, foolish old woman.

The sadness of the lives of the two messengers at La Salette does not negate the apparition. Indeed, it serves to repeat the theme of La Salette — heaven's sorrow at the sins of mankind.

September 19, 1846, was the eve of the feast of Our Lady of Sorrows. Maximin Giraud, age eleven, and Melanie Mathieu, age fourteen, were tending cows in a field in the French Alps in the parish of La Salette. The children had only met the day before, so there was no chance of their making up the incredible story that they told of the events of that day.

Melanie was one of eight children of a very poor family from Corps. With the specter of starvation always present she had been sent into the streets to beg as a young child, and had been hired out to work from the age of seven. Melanie had never been to school, and although her mother had taught her the Our Father and the Hail Mary, she rarely went to church and had never made her First Communion.

Maximin's family was barely better off than Melanie's. His father worked hard as a wheelright, but spent most of his pay on liquor at the local bars. The child did not get along with his stepmother and spent most of his time playing and staying out of her way. Like Melanie, he had never attended school. He, too, knew only a few prayers, and did not attend church.

Melanie and Maximin were typical of many of the inhabitants of the area. After the French Revolution, this part of France had never returned to the Faith. Only a few old people attended Mass. Sunday was seen by most of the people as only another working day. Days of fast and abstinence were ignored. Blasphemy was common.

At the ringing of the Angelus, Maximin and Melanie took their small herd to water them in a small ravine. There were three sources of water there: one for the cows, one for the herders, and a third called "the little fountain," which gave water only after heavy snows or rains and now was completely dry. After the cows had been watered, the children sat to eat their simple lunch of bread and cheese. In the warmth of the sun, they stretched out for a short nap, sleeping longer than had they intended. Awakening, Melanie realized they had overslept, and the children rushed to find the cows. Fortunately, they were all grazing peacefully together. With a sigh of relief, Melanie returned to the ravine to retrieve the knapsacks in which the children had carried their lunch.

There in the ravine, only a few steps away, blazed a great circle of light. The astounded child looked at it wide-eyed. Quickly she called Maximin, who saw it too. Both children were frightened, although Maximin told her that if it attempted to hurt them he would hit it with his staff.

Before their eyes, the globe of light grew in intensity and brilliance. They would have fled in fear except that they noticed that the globe was opening up and little by little they could discern within it the figure of a woman. The woman was seated, bent forward. Her face was inclined in her hands, her elbows resting on her knees, and she was weeping.

The luminous figure than arose, her head tilted a little to one side, her arms crossed on her breast. The beauty of her

55

face was extraordinary, despite the tears. A white headdress covered her hair, clung to her cheeks, and hid her neck. A towering crown rested on her brow, edged below with roses of many colors that gave off shimmering rays of light. She wore a long white dress with full sleeves, sprinkled with bursts of light. She wore a small shawl trimmed with roses which seemed to form golden lace. Along the hem of the shawl were metal links, not joined in a chain but distinctly separated one from the next. Tied about her waist was a large apron, yellow and glittering as gold. She wore white slippers decorated with clusters of pearls, gold buckles, and the same sort of roses as those on the crown and shawl. She wore a crucifix hanging from a chain, and the children later described the figure on the cross as of fire. To the left of the crucifix was a hammer; to the right a pair of pliers, half open.

Then the woman spoke gently, "Come to me, my children, do not be afraid. I am here to tell you something of the greatest importance."

Their fright disappeared, and the children stepped forward, descending into the ravine and crossing the bed of the stream. The beautiful lady moved toward them until they, too, were enveloped in the globe of light.

Crystalline tears flowed constantly from the beautiful eyes. "If my people will not obey, I shall be compelled to loose my Son's arm. It is so heavy, so pressing that I can no longer restrain it. How long have I suffered for you! If my Son is not to cast you off, I am obliged to entreat Him without ceasing. But you take no least heed of that. No matter how well you pray in future, no matter how well you act, you will never be able to make up to me what I have endured in your behalf.

"I have appointed you six days for working. The seventh

I have reserved for myself, and no one will give it to me. This it is which causes the weight of my Son's arm to be so crushing.

"The cart drivers cannot swear without bringing in my Son's name. These are the two things that make my Son's arm so burdensome.

"If the harvest is spoiled, it is your fault. I warned you last year by means of the potatoes. You paid no attention. Quite the reverse, when you discovered that the potatoes had decayed, you swore, you abused my Son's name. They will continue to be spoiled, and by Christmas time this year there will be none left."

Melanie looked inquiringly at Maximin, for the lady was speaking French and Melanie barely understood the language. Both Melanie and Maximin spoke a local patois.

The woman spoke again, "Ah, you do not understand French, my children. Well, then, listen. I shall put it differently." Then, in the local patois she repeated what she had said. She continued, "If you have grain, it will do no good to sow it, for what you sow the beasts will eat, and whatever part of it springs up will crumble into dust when you thresh it.

"A great famine is coming. But before that happens, the children under seven years of age will be seized with trembling and die in the arms of the parents holding them. The grown-ups will pay for their sins by hunger. The grapes will rot, and the walnuts will turn bad."

The woman broke off here and began speaking to Maximin. Melanie could not hear a word, although she could see the beautiful lady's lips moving. Then she turned to Melanie and gave her a secret which Maximin, try as he might, could not overhear.

On a different note, the lady began speaking again to

both children. "If people are converted, the rocks will become piles of wheat and it will be found that the potatoes have sown themselves."

Looking searchingly at the two poor youngsters, the woman interrupted her message to ask, "Do you say your prayers well, my children?"

They replied, "No, Madame, hardly at all."

"Ah, my children, it is very important to do so, at night and in the morning. When you don't have time, at least say an 'Our Father' and a 'Hail Mary,' and when you can, say more."

She returned again to the main theme. "Only a few rather old women go to Mass in the summer. Everyone else works every Sunday all summer long. And in winter, when they don't know what to do with themselves, they go to Mass only to scoff at religion. During Lent, they go to the butcher shop like dogs."

She interrupted again to ask the children if they knew what spoiled wheat was like. When they replied in the negative, she reminded Maximin of a time when his father had showed him spoiled wheat and talked with him about his worries over crop failure and starvation. It amazed the boy, who had forgotten the incident, that the beautiful lady knew so much.

Again the woman spoke in French. These were her last words, "Well, my children, you will make this known to all my people."

She turned from the children, stepped across the stream bed, and without looking back repeated her final words. Slowly she walked the length of the ravine and up the slope. The children, enthralled, accompanied her, Melanie a little ahead, Maximin a little behind. She appeared to be gliding above the ground, as the grass did not even bend. At the top

OUR LADY OF LA SALETTE: one of several statues depicting attitudes of the Blessed Virgin at the mountain shrine in France

of the ravine she paused, and then she gracefully rose into the air. She looked up to heaven and ceased to weep. A final glance over the world and she began to disappear. The apparition faded into the upper air, leaving a path of radiance, which vanished without trace within a few seconds.

When the children arrived at the respective houses of their employers, Melanie went to bed the cattle for the night, and Maximin, who was not assigned this chore, went in to supper. When his employer, Pierre Selme, questioned him about why he had not returned to the field in the afternoon, Maximin told him of being detained by the beautiful woman. In disbelief, Selme determined that they would go to Baptiste Pra's house and ask Melanie for her account, as she was known to be of a more solemn and truthful nature than the flighty Maximin. On their arrival, the boy repeated his story. Grandmother Pra was the first to recognize that it must have been an apparition of the Blessed Virgin, and she went to the barn to hear Melanie's story. The word passed quickly from house to house in the little hamlet, and it was determined that the children should go in the morning and tell their story to the priest at La Salette. Some of their listeners had disbelieved, some had scoffed, but all agreed that it was a matter for the Church.

The next morning, the children presented themselves at the rectory. The housekeeper refused to show them in to see the priest until they told her what was so important that they should be allowed to interrupt Father Perrin that early in the morning. From his nearby study, the priest overheard their arrival and quietly slipped in to listen to the incredible tale the children were telling. At its conclusion, he began to weep, and he told the children that they were fortunate to have had a vision of the Blessed Virgin. As it was time for Mass, Maximin left to join his employer for the trip home.

He had been substituting for Selme's regular herder that week, and this was the day appointed for his return to his own home. Melanie, who had so rarely attended Mass, slipped unnoticed into the back of the church. She was horrified to find that the devout priest, weeping grievously, was telling the people the story of the events of the day before.

After Mass, Melanie hurried back to Pra's. But she was to know no peace. Soon the mayor of Ablandins arrived and began to question her. Time and again she repeated her story, never deviating from it. No matter how tricky his questions, he was not able to catch her in a contradiction. Neither threats of jail nor promises of money would make the girl change her determination to say what the lady had told her to say.

Maximin's story, too, was rejected by his family, except his grandmother. Again, dire threats and inducements could not deter the child from his determination to tell the truth.

On hearing the story, Father Melin, the parish priest of Corps, determined to investigate properly. He accompanied the children to the spot of the apparition, along with four observant parishioners. Here he became convinced by the children's actions and attitudes that their story indeed was a true one. Most properly, however, he determined to report to the bishop, whom he trusted to carry out the correct canonical investigation. At this visit, it was noticed that the dried-up spring, which so rarely gave water, was flowing freely.

Father Melin returned to Corps with a bottle of this water which he gave to a parishioner of his who had been critically ill for some time.

This parishioner drank some of the water daily, and made a novena to the Blessed Virgin. On the ninth day, she was completely restored to health. Properly, the priest called this only an "extraordinary" happening, not referring to it as a miracle.

The time had come for Father Melin to report to the bishop. He wrote him a long letter setting forth the children's stories and all the facts. He concluded with the words, "I submit these details to the bishop, who will give what orders he thinks best. It is the view of the people, naturally, that the Mother of God has come to warn the world before her Son rains down punishments. My own conviction, in the light of all the evidence I have been able to gather, is indentical with the people's, and I believe that this warning is a great favor from heaven. I have no need of further wonders to believe. But my intense desire would be that God, in His mercy, should work some new marvel to confirm the first."

Both of Father Melin's wishes were heeded. First, the bishop began a lengthy, exacting, and proper investigation. Secondly, new marvels confirming the visit of Our Lady began to pour in. A number of miraculous healings occurred. Best of all, the people of the area began to heed the warning and return to the practice of their religion.

At last, the bishop instigated a full juridical inquiry in July of 1847 that was to last four years. At long last, he drew up the doctrinal pronouncement on La Salette, which he signed on the fifth anniversary of the apparition, September 19, 1851. It was examined by Rome and then printed and distributed in all of the churches under Bishop de Bruillard's authority. In it, he declared that the apparition had all the marks of truth, and authorized the cult of Our Lady of La Salette. A basilica was built in her honor at the site, and successive popes have given statements of credence to the cult.

St. John Bosco wrote of La Salette. To him it was clear that Our Lady asked reform of men's thinking and living.

He said, "Let us so act that this will be to us a source of graces and blessings, serving to rouse in us a faith which is vital, a faith which is efficacious, a faith which leads us to do good and avoid evil, that we may be worthy of the divine mercy in time and in eternity."

Another who found inspiration in La Salette was St. Peter Julian Eymard. He recognized Mary's call for reparation, and here on her mountain he was mysteriously moved to begin his work for perpetual adoration of Christ in the Blessed Sacrament in reparation for the evils in which so many lives were bogged down.

Other priests were influenced by Our Lady of La Salette. Indeed, an entire order dedicated to her under this title was begun with a specific mission to work for reconciliation. These priests have spread throughout the world, carrying Our Lady's message to the millions.

After Lourdes, Bernadette went on to become a great saint. A cause has been begun for two of the little seers of Fatima. On the other hand, the children of La Salette did not go on to become great saints. They did, however, fulfill their mission, to make known Our Lady's words. Their task was then finished. Unfortunately, for years they were not able to find the only privacy and peace available to them — the privacy of the grace and the peace of eternity. Unprotected by the peace of any cloister, and true to their own natures, their lives were disappointing to those who mistake the call to perform a specific service with the guarantee of a special sanctity.

In today's age, with our increased knowledge of how to deal with and treat mental instability and neuroticism, perhaps both Melanie and Maximin would have fared better. A clearer understanding of their personalities and proper intervention by Church authorities might have prevented much of the pain of their lives after the apparition. Not so in the mid-nineteenth century. With the exception of the beautiful thirty minutes when they were privileged to behold the wonderful visitor from heaven, and the joy of being chosen to communicate her message to the world, the entire lives of Melanie Mathieu and Maximin Giraud are to be pitied. Both began in poverty and ignorance, and both ended in mental instability. It is to their credit that they never deviated from the facts of their initial story of the apparition. As one of the main parts of the message of La Salette is the emphasis on mercy, who can doubt that the divine mercy was granted to Melanie and Maximin? The tears of Our Lady of La Salette, prompted by mercy, were wept for them and for all mankind.

Our Lady of La Salette, hear my cries of repentance. Help me keep my resolve to turn away from my sins which so offend your divine Son. Just as my sins served as the hammer which drove the nails into Our Lord, let my repentance serve as the pliers which pull them out again and release Him from the cross.

Our Lady of Lavang

THE FIRST Catholic missionaries arrived in Indo-China (Vietnam) in 1533. A scant hundred years later, there were over a hundred thousand Catholics in the area. Seminaries were established, and by 1668 two native priests were ordained. A group of women Religious was formed in 1670 which is still active today.

Throughout history, Catholics have been persecuted for their faith. Vietnam was no exception. Severe persecutions broke out in 1698. In the eigtheenth century there were three more persecutions. And again in the nineteenth century there were persecutions. The sturdy Vietnamese Catholics stood firm, in spite of the danger. Over one hundred thousand Catholics were martyred in the mid-1800s alone. Today, under the communist regime, the bishops and priests are still harassed. Fragmentary reports on the status of the Church since the war are not encouraging. In spite of this, pilgrims flock annually to the shrine of Our Lady of Lavang. This shrine was established in 1800 at Hué, near the center of the country.

At the end of the seventeenth century, the persecution of Catholics in central Vietnam was so severe that many of the people fled to a remote jungle area in the mountains near Lavang. They wished to be free to practice their religion, as well as to save their lives.

One evening as the community was reciting the Rosary

*OUR LADY OF LAVANG: Statue commemorating miraculous
apparitions is similar to Our Lady of Victory in Paris*

The South Vietnamese government issued a stamp honoring "Duc Me La-Vang" (Blessed Mother of Lavang) before the fall of Saigon

together, there was an apparition of a beautiful lady holding a little child in her arms, with angels surrounding her. The lady was dressed simply but wore a crown. The people recognized the beautiful Lady as the Queen of Heaven. She spoke to the people in the loving tones of a mother. She encouraged and comforted them. Displaying a tender concern for her children, she taught the people how to make medicines from the plants and herbs that grew in the area. She also promised her protection to any who would come to that particular site to pray. Unlike her messages at Fatima and Lourdes, those brought by the Lady of Lavang were only messages of comfort, not warnings. She simply expressed her tender mother's care for her persecuted children. The apparition was seen again a number of times.

The people of Lavang built a simple church of leaves and rice straw and dedicated it to their Mother Mary. Devotion to her grew, and a number of miraculous cures and favors were reported. Through other persecutions, the Lavang area continued to be a sanctuary for oppressed Catholics.

In 1805, officers of the Vietnamese emperor began an anticolonial movement. They were determined to rid the country of all Catholics. No longer was Lavang safe. Thirty Catholics were put to death by the emperor's soldiers right at the door of their little church. The church was burned, although not by one of the soldiers. The soldiers had heard of the miraculous deeds at Lavang and were frightened to destroy the chapel. Amazingly, the altar and the chandeliers, both made of wood, survived the fire. The people then rebuilt their beloved shrine. On the site where the original apparitions took place, a new brick church was begun in 1885. It was completed in 1900, and in 1901 the first annual celebration of the Shrine of Our Lady of Lavang took place. Over 130,000 Catholics from all over the country participated. Devotion to Our Lady of Lavang grew rapidly, and by 1925 it was necessary to enlarge the complex because of the throngs of worshipers. This church was completed in 1928. Many non-Christians acknowledged that there was something special about this place. In the early 1920s, the emperor of Vietnam fell ill. A non-Christian, he sent one of his Christian ministers to pray for him at the shrine. He recovered speedily.

During World War II, Vietnam was a battleground for the Japanese and the French. After this, the French and the communists, known as the Vietcong, battled until 1954 when they split the country into two governments. Almost a million people fled from the communists in the North. At this time, Lavang became a center of pilgrimage. In 1961, the conference of the Vietnamese bishops made the church the national shrine of the country. In August of 1963, Pope Paul VI conferred on the church the title of Basilica of Our Lady of Lavang.

By April of 1975, when South Vietnam fell under the control of the communists, the Lavang complex had enlarged to include a retreat center, a hospitality center, an outdoor amphitheater, and a beautiful statue of Mary commemorating her apparitions.

The Vietnamese people have always had a special devotion to the Blessed Mother. They carry this love for her with them, wherever they go. They trust their Mother to keep them in her loving care, just as she cared for those who were privileged to see her at the apparitions at Lavang.

Our Lady of the Miraculous Medal

"CATHERINE, Catherine, wake up. Come to the chapel; the Blessed Virgin is waiting for you."

Sleepily, Sister Catherine Labouré, a novice of the Sisters of Charity at the motherhouse on the Rue de Bac in Paris, France, opened her eyes.

"About half past eleven [July 18, 1830], I heard myself called by my name. I looked in the direction of the voice and I drew the curtain. I saw a child, four or five years old, dressed in white, who [told me to come into the chapel]. Immediately the thought came to me: 'But I shall be heard.' The child replied: 'Be calm . . . everyone is asleep; come, I am waiting for you.'

"I hurriedly dressed and went to the side of the child. I followed him wherever he went. The lights were lit everywhere.

"When we reached the chapel, the door opened as soon as the child touched it with the tip of his finger. The candles were burning as at midnight Mass. However, I did not see the Blessed Virgin. The child led me to the sanctuary and I knelt down there. Toward midnight, the child said: 'Here is the Blessed Virgin!' I heard a noise like the rustle of a silk dress . . . [and] a beautiful lady sat down in Father Director's chair. The child repeated in a strong voice: 'Here is the Blessed Virgin!' Then I flung myself at her feet on the steps of the altar and put my hands on her knees.

71

"I do not know how long I remained there; it seemed but a moment, the sweetest of my life.

"The Holy Virgin told me how I should act toward my director and confided several things to me. . . ."

On hearing these words, the young novice's spiritual director, Father Aladel, a young Lazarist, could not be blamed for thinking that Sister Catherine was possibly the victim of an overactive imagination.

Later, Catherine wrote of the things the virgin confided to her that night. " 'The good God, my child, wishes to entrust you with a mission. It will be the cause of much suffering to you, but you will overcome this, knowing that what you do is for the glory of God. You will be contradicted, but you will have the grace to bear it; do not fear. You will see certain things: give an account of them. You will be inspired in your prayers.

" 'The times are evil, misfortunes will fall upon France; the throne will be overthrown; the entire world will be overcome by evils of all kinds . . . but . . . come to the foot of this altar; there, graces will be poured on all those who ask for them with confidence and fervor. They will be poured out on the great and humble. . . .' "

Catherine's mission was revealed to her on November 27, 1830. While at community prayer, Catherine again saw the Blessed Virgin. She was standing dressed in a robe of white silk with her feet resting on a globe. In her hands she held a smaller globe, and her eyes were raised toward heaven.

"Then suddenly, I saw rings on her fingers, covered with jewels . . . from which came beautiful rays. . . . At this moment . . . she lowered her eyes and looked at me, and an interior voice spoke to me: 'This globe which you see represents the entire world, particularly France, and each person in particular. This is a symbol of the graces which I shed on those who ask me.'

"At this moment, where I was or was not I do not know, an oval shape formed around the Blessed Virgin, and on it were written these words in letters of gold: 'O Mary conceived without sin, pray for us who have recourse to thee.'

"Then a voice was heard to say: 'Have a medal struck after this model. Those who wear it will receive great graces; abundant graces will be given to those who have confidence.' (Some of the precious stones gave forth no ray of light.) 'Those jewels which are in shadow represent the graces which people forget to ask me for.'

"Suddenly, the oval seemed to turn. I saw the reverse of the medal: the letter M surmounted by a cross, and below it two hearts, one crowned with a crown of thorns, and the other pierced by a sword. I seemed to hear a voice which said to me: 'The M and the two hearts say enough.' "

After this last account, Father Aladel still had his doubts, but he requested an interview with the archbishop of Paris. The archbishop could find nothing against the Faith in the idea, and authorized the medal to be struck. In May of 1832, the first medals were distributed, and soon there was a flood of reported cures and conversions. So many, in fact, that people soon began calling it the "Miraculous Medal."

On July 27, 1947, Pope Pius XII canonized St. Catherine Labouré and called her the "Saint of Silence." Through obedience, Catherine had spoken to no one except her confessor of her remarkable visions through the years. Shortly before her death at the age of seventy, the Virgin released her from her silence, and for the first time she told the story of her miraculous apparitions to her superior. In 1866, some months before her death, she wrote an account of these in

OUR LADY OF THE MIRACULOUS MEDAL: Chapel
on the Rue de Bac, Paris, emblazons the prayer "O Mary
conceived without sin, pray for us who have recourse to thee"

*Statue portrays Catherine Labouré's vision
of Mary showering her graces all over the world*

her own handwriting, which is today preserved at the shrine.

Each of the predictions that the Blessed Mother had made to St. Catherine Labouré had come true. Misfortunes had befallen France and the entire world. The French throne had indeed been overthrown. Catherine had been disbelieved and contradicted, yet her mission had been completed.

The Miraculous Medal became a sign for the renewal of devotion to Our Lady and for an evangelical revival. Today, many visitors throng to the tiny chapel where Catherine saw the Blessed Mother. Millions of Catholics worldwide wear the Miraculous Medal as a reminder of the blessings Our Lady is waiting for them to request.

Our Lady of the Miraculous Medal, help me remember that you stand ready to shower graces on me, if only I ask for them. Let me pray, as you taught, "O Mary conceived without sin, pray for us who have recourse to thee."

Our Lady of Mount Carmel

DEVOTION TO Our Lady of Mt. Carmel is one of the most ancient, and strongest, of the Marian devotions. Although Carmel is a place, it is more — an entire manner of living. The spirituality of this devotion can properly extend to any Christian, in any walk of life.

In the spirituality of Carmel, there is a threefold purpose: (1) to follow Jesus Christ as brothers and sisters of the Blessed Virgin Mary, called together by the Holy Spirit; (2) to live as Elijah in the presence of God; (3) to serve the needs of the Church and one another in love. An ancient command from Mt. Carmel in the Holy Land reads, "Keep Mary in mind, and Jesus will grow in your heart."

Carmel reminds us that the true spirit of devotion to Mary lies in our working with and through her to attain Christian perfection . . . to God, through Mary, for love.

The Carmelite order has been abundantly blessed with mystical writers. Each has given insights to the spiritual life. St. Teresa of Avila saw the spiritual life as a way of perfection. St. John of the Cross saw it as an ascent to Mount Carmel. St. Thérèse of Lisieux saw it as a "little way." One devout Carmelite writer expresses the place of Mary when he says, "You will become better because she teaches the way of God."

Carmel is a place name, bound up in the Bible with Elijah. It is a mountain twenty miles from Nazareth on the

OUR LADY OF MOUNT CARMEL: miraculous painting preserved at a Carmelite church in Italy

border of Samaria and Galilee. The name Carmel comes from the Hebrew words for garden and vine of God. The place was famed for its beauty and luxurious vegetation, and became known as a symbol of grace and blessing. Here God intervened through Elijah the Prophet, in the ninth century before Christ, and renewed His covenant with the Israelites. With the Crusades, in the late 1100s, came Westerners who began on Mt. Carmel a contemplative life which the Holy See approved in 1226. This group called themselves the Order of the Brothers of the Blessed Virgin Mary of Mt. Carmel. After the Crusades, they became mendicant friars and many returned to the West. They took the patronage of Mary home with them, spreading devotion to her wherever they went.

Traditionally, a special grace of the Virgin toward the Carmelites was her promise attached to the brown scapular of their order. The prior general of the Carmelite Order, St. Simon Stock, appealed to Our Lady for assistance at a crucial time, begging her for a special privilege for the Brothers who bore her name. In 1251, while he was at prayer, Our Lady appeared to him at Aylesford, England, holding the scapular and promising, "This shall be a sign for you and for all Carmelites. Whosoever dies in this shall not suffer eternal fire." Even though there are historical difficulties, a case can be made for the story of the vision. The understanding of the scapular devotion is, however, the most important part. The scapular is a miniature habit, a highly indulgenced sacramental, and a privileged sign of affiliation with the Carmelite Order, which commits the wearer to follow Our Lady's way of life. The wearing of the scapular is not merely a pious superstition, nor should the scapular itself be considered some type of holy "good-luck charm." It is a sacramental for constantly inspiring the wearer to trust totally in God as Mary did when she said, "Be it done to me according to your word." It commands the wearer to follow Our Lord as Mary commanded at Cana, "Do whatever He tells you."

The scapular devotion to Our Lady of Mt. Carmel was extended to the laity and spread rapidly in the late 1400s.

The order of Carmelites spread and grew. Their devotion to Mary as the model of contemplative prayer also grew. When St. Teresa of Avila was asked what she did in order to think of God always, she replied, "It is not difficult — we naturally think of someone we love." Through the centuries, the devotion to Mary remained strong, and the character of this devotion was Christocentric. In spite of expansion, growth, changes, and reforms, the Carmelites' devotion to Mary remained a central part of their spirituality.

To our present day, Carmelites have written about and lived their Marian devotion. St. Thérèse of Lisieux wrote of Mary as the Gospel woman of faith. Her writings have a mass appeal because they are simple and easily understood by everyone, as in her "little way." Blessed Elizabeth of the Trinity, a cloistered French Carmelite who made the Holy Trinity the center of her spirituality, thought of Mary as the "Gateway to Heaven." Blessed Edith Stein, a brilliant German philosopher and convert, spent her last days imitating the Motherhood of Mary. As Sister Benedicta of the Cross, O.C.D., she was sent to Auschwitz in 1942 and died in the gas chamber there. Until her death, she mothered the children of the Jews and others condemned with her who were too frightened to comfort their children themselves. Known as "the dangerous little friar," the Dutch Carmelite journalist Blessed Titus Brandsma was sent to Dachau for his stand against the Nazi press. His last days were witnessed by a fallen-away Catholic nurse, who administered the final, lethal injection of poison which ended his earthly life. To her he gave his last possession, his rosary, telling her that if she could not remember the prayers she only need remember the words "Pray for us sinners." The Venerable Maria Teresa Quevado of Spain (d. 1950) explained her Marian devotion simply. "I love Our Lord with all my heart, but He wants me to love Our Lady in a special way, and to go to Him with my hand in Mary's." Shortly before her death, she seemed to see someone in the room with her, and she whispered "How beautiful, Mary, how beautiful you are."

Our Lady of Mt. Carmel, as you swaddled your infant Son Jesus, protected Him as a child, loved and served Him through His adulthood, and grieved for Him as you shared His crucifixion as co-redemptorix, remember us, your children, who appeal to you. Grant us perseverance that we, with you, may ascend the heights of Carmel.

OUR LADY OF POMPEII: Mother and Child in miraculous painting retrieved from a junk shop see kneeling figures of Sts. Dominic and Catherine of Siena (latter painted over St. Rose)

Our Lady of the Rosary of Pompeii

"THAT PICTURE is so ugly that it must have been painted purposely to destroy devotion to Our Lady!" So spoke the Countess Marianna di Fusco on her first glimpse of the painting of Our Lady which was to help increase devotion to the Rosary in the desolate valley of Pompeii.

Blessed Bartolo Longo, while visiting the valley of Pompeii on business in 1872, was shocked and filled with great pity at the ignorance, poverty, and lack of religion of the inhabitants of the area. His generous heart was moved, and he promised Our Lady to do all in his power to promote devotion to the Rosary among the people of the area. To this end, he set up rosary festivals with games, races, and even a lottery to attract the people.

In order to encourage the people, he determined to purchase a picture to be exposed for veneration by the peasants at the end of a three-day mission. By canon law, the picture had to be a painting in oils or on wood.

In vain, Blessed Bartolo and a priest friend scoured Naples for a painting of the Virgin with her rosary. At last, a Dominican sister offered them a large painting which had been bought at a junk shop for three francs. Seeing their hesitation, she told the men not to hesitate about taking the picture and predicted that it would work miracles. Rather than disappoint the people of Pompeii by returning empty-handed, Bartolo accepted the picture and made arrangements for a wagoner to transport it to Pompeii.

Blessed Bartolo himself described the picture, which was dilapidated, wrinkled, soiled, and torn — "Not only was it worm-eaten, but the face of the Madonna was that of a coarse, rough country woman . . . a piece of canvas was missing just above her head . . . her mantle was cracked. Nothing can be said of the hideousness of the other figures. St. Dominic looked like a street idiot. To Our Lady's left was a St. Rose. This latter I had changed later into a St. Catherine of Siena. . . . I hesitated whether to refuse the gift or to accept. I had promised a picture unconditionally for that evening. I took it."

The wagoner arrived at the chapel door with the large painting wrapped in a sheet, and on top of a load of manure which he was delivering to a nearby field! Thus did Our Lady of Pompeii arrive in the valley which would become one of the major places of pilgrimage in honor of Our Lady.

At first, everyone who saw the picture was disappointed. An artist refurbished the unsightly canvas and ornamented it with diamonds donated by the faithful. A crown was placed on the head of the Madonna, and the painting was solemnly mounted on a throne of marble imported from Lourdes.

Bartolo later commented, "There is something about that picture which impresses the soul not by its artistic perfection but by a mysterious charm that impels one to kneel and pray with tears."

Immediately on its exposition, the picture became a veritable fountain of miracles.

First, a young epileptic girl in Naples was restored to health on the very day that the picture was re-exposed for veneration. Her aunt had heard of the plans to form a rosary confraternity in Pompeii and vowed to assist in the building of the church if the child got well. Next, a young woman dying in agony was completely recovered, immediately after her relatives had made similar promises to Our Lady of Pompeii. A Jesuit priest who had been persuaded by the Countess di Fusco to put his faith in the Virgin of Pompeii was cured of cancer immediately, and on the following Feast of the Holy Rosary he sang the Mass and acknowledged his cure from the pulpit at Pompeii. In less than ten years, over nine hundred forty cures were reported at the shrine.

Today the picture is mounted in a frame of gold and is encrusted with diamonds and precious gems which hide all but the faces of the saints and the Holy Child. Daily, pilgrims plead with Our Lady here for her graces and her favors. In this valley where once a pagan religion thrived, Our Lady reigns over her subjects, whom she calls to adoration of her Son.

Queen of Pompeii, help us to remember that true beauty lies not in external appearances, but rather in what comes from within. Let us never forget that God loves, above all things, the beauty of each individual human soul.

Our Lady of Prompt Succor

I N 1812, A terrible fire ravaged the city of New Orleans, Louisiana. A high wind rapidly drove the flames toward the Ursuline convent, and the order was given for the nuns to leave the cloister. Sister Anthony, a lay sister, placed a small statue of Our Lady of Prompt Succor on a windowsill facing the fire, and she and Mother St. Michel prayed, "Our Lady of Prompt Succor, we are lost unless you hasten to our help." Instantly the wind changed, and the convent was out of danger. Once again, Our Lady had hastened to set her seal of approval on the work of the Ursulines and the spread of the faith in the South.

The Ursuline Monastery of New Orleans was founded under the auspices of King Louis XV of France by a band of French Ursulines in 1727. Soon after their arrival, the nuns began to teach the children of the colonists, to instruct the Indian and Negro races, and to nurse the sick in a hospital placed under their care. Other sisters came from France, and in 1763 when Louisiana became a Spanish possession, Spanish sisters helped to carry on the work. In 1800, when Louisiana again became French territory, the Spanish sisters left for Cuba, fearing that the horrors of the recent French Revolution would be repeated in the colonies. Thus by 1803 only seven Ursulines remained to carry on the boarding school, day school, orphanage, courses of instruction for the Indians and Negroes, and the nursing of the

OUR LADY OF PROMPT SUCCOR:
Doll-like figure, patroness of Louisiana,
is venerated at the national votive shrine
of the Ursuline Sisters in New Orleans

sick. The superior appealed to a cousin of hers in France, Mother St. Michel, for aid and personnel.

Mother St. Michel had been driven from her convent by the Reign of Terror, and as soon as the first indication of religious tolerance appeared, she had, with another young woman, opened a boarding school for young girls which was beginning to realize all the hopes the bishop of her diocese had for it. Her bishop was happy to have such a zealous worker among his flock and did not want to lose her. On receiving the appeal from her cousin in New Orleans, Mother St. Michel asked her spiritual director for his advice. He demurred. On direct appeal to the bishop, the answer came, "Only the Pope can give you authorization." This reply amounted almost to a definite "no," as the Pope was in Rome, a virtual prisoner of Napoleon, and his jailors were under strict injunction not to allow him to correspond with anyone. Additionally, there was no reliable way of sending messages. Nonetheless, Mother St. Michel wrote her request, concluding, "Most Holy Father, I appeal to your apostolic tribunal. I am ready to submit to your decision. Speak. Faith teaches me that you are the voice of the Lord. I await your orders. 'Go' or 'Stay' from Your Holiness will be the same to me."

The letter had been written for three months, but no opportunity had presented itself to send it. One day, as she was praying before a statue of Mary, Mother felt inspired to call on the Queen of Heaven with these words, "O Most Holy Virgin Mary, if you obtain a prompt and favorable answer to my letter, I promise to have you honored in New Orleans under the title of Our Lady of Prompt Succor."

That Mother St. Michel's trustful prayer was pleasing to Our Lady and that she wished to be honored in the New World under this title are shown by the prompt and favorable reply the nun received. The letter was dispatched on March 19, 1809, and the reply is dated in Rome on April 28.

That the reply directed Mother to place herself at the head of religious aspirants and go to Louisiana is miraculous in itself. The Pope was well aware of the need for workers such as Mother St. Michel in France. Many would be needed to regenerate what the Revolution had torn down. Nonetheless, he gave his approval of her voyage, and her bishop acknowledged that his hopes to keep her in France were defeated. He requested the privilege of blessing the statue of Our Lady which Mother St. Michel had commissioned according to her promise.

On the arrival of the pious missionaries in New Orleans in December of 1810, this precious statue was solemnly installed in the convent chapel, and from that time the veneration of Mary under the title of Our Lady of Prompt Succor has been constantly growing and spreading all across the United States.

The victory of Andrew Jackson's American forces over the British in the Battle of New Orleans in 1815 is another favor attributed to the all-powerful intercession of Our Lady of Prompt Succor. Before the battle, the terror-stricken, weeping mothers, sisters, and daughters of Jackson's valiant little band spent the night in prayer in the chapel of the convent. They begged Our Lady for help for Jackson's men on the plains of Chalmette. On the morning of January 8, the statue of Our Lady of Prompt Succor was moved above the main altar, and the Ursulines made a vow to have a Mass of Thanksgiving sung annually should the Americans be victorious. At the moment of Communion, a courier rushed into the chapel announcing the enemy's defeat. Jackson himself acknowledged divine intervention on his behalf, and he came in person with his staff to thank the nuns for their prayers. The vow made by the Ursulines has been faithfully kept for over one hundred seventy years.

The chronicles of the Ursuline monastery record numerous favors, both spiritual and temporal, wrought through the intercession of Our Lady of Prompt Succor. Rome has officially approved the devotion. By papal decree in 1851, Pius IX authorized the celebration of the Feast of Our Lady of Prompt Succor and the singing of the yearly Mass of Thanksgiving on January 8. In 1894, Pope Leo XIII indulgenced the confraternity, and in 1897 raised it to the rank of an archconfraternity. The statue was solemnly crowned by the papal delegate in 1895. This was the first ceremony of this type in the United States. In 1928, a new shrine in Our Lady's honor was consecrated, and by a decree of the Sacred Congregation of Rites, the Holy See approved and confirmed the choice of Our Lady of Prompt Succor as the principal patroness of the City of New Orleans and the State of Louisiana. The patronal feast was set for January 15. In 1960, the solemn sesquicentennial of the arrival of Our Lady of Prompt Succor in Louisiana was celebrated.

When we invoke Our Lady under this title, we are telling her that our needs are great and pressing, and that we hope and expect much from her. Our confidence need know no bounds, as Our Lady's power equals her love. May devotion to Mary under this hope-inspiring title continue to grow and spread.

Our Lady of Prompt Succor, you know that my needs are great and pressing. Hasten to help me, and always give me the grace to accept whatever God's will for my life is.

Our Lady of the Rockies

NEAR THE EAST Coast of the United States, the Statue of Liberty stands as a beacon of American freedom. High atop a ridge of the Continental Divide, overlooking Butte, Montana, another metal lady stands, a symbol of love and universal motherhood.

Our Lady of the Rockies is a ninety-foot-tall statue fabricated of sixty tons of steel and painted white. Her hands open wide as if in blessing on those in the town below. The statue is dedicated to Our Blessed Mother and to mothers everywhere. Built through love, she stands as a beacon to love and a reminder of promises kept.

In 1979, Bob O'Bill, then a mineworker for Anaconda, promised to put up a small statue in honor of Mary and mothers everywhere if his wife, Joyce, recovered from an illness. Reluctant to speak about the original request, today Joyce merely says, "He thought I was sicker than I really was." She, as do many others who worked on the project, prefers that the monument's history be remembered as a symbol of all promises kept, not just one. A symbol of what can result when many people pool their talents and resources and work in unity. Although the O'Bills are Catholic, many of the workers on the project were of other religions. Joe Roberts says that the statue was put up for "love — love of wives and mothers everywhere." He and the members of the nonprofit Our Lady of the Rockies Foundation believe that Mary typifies motherhood to every race or creed since the beginning of time. They ask, "What mother ever gave more? Mary gave mankind a most beautiful gift in her firstborn Son. That is the reality of love and motherhood that we honor."

One man's goal became the goal of many. Many of the workers remembered times when prayers had been answered and when they had forgotten the promises they had made.

As Roberts put it, "[We remembered] promises made and broken over many years, to wives, mothers, friends, and, above all, to God. . . . Many of us realized that we were bankrupt with unfulfilled pledges and promises made but not paid."

The project grew by leaps and bounds. People donated mining claims to secure the site; Anaconda donated road-building machinery, and Ideal Basic Industries provided the cement for the base. A road to connect the site with the existing road was built. Governmental regulatory agency rules were learned and followed. A nonprofit corporation was established to ensure that no individual profited from the project. Many local businesses donated supplies and equipment. A majority of the money from actual cash donations went to purchase diesel fuel to run donated heavy equipment. Butte citizens contributed years of engineering skills, time, and talents. As Roberts put it, "The blood, sweat, and tears came from the community."

Donations have come from almost every country of the world. At the last, the United States government contributed by loaning, at cost only, a special helicopter to airlift the parts of the massive statue to its final site. Best of all, the project grew into one of unity of different races and creeds, a joint effort to remind Americans of one of the

OUR LADY OF THE ROCKIES, a community project, stands on the exact Continental Divide overlooking U.S. Interstate Highway 15 near Bute, Mont. (photo by Cathy Tilzey)

basic principals this country was based on . . . "United we stand."

Actual construction began in 1983. Although the statue is the largest piece of art in Montana, it was designed by a working craftsman, not a sculptor. In the planning stages, the group wanted to search for an artist who would donate his or her talents. Designs submitted, however, presented technical problems. Leroy Lee, a machinist and welder who worked for Roberts, was asked if he could design and build the statue. Lee was skeptical, but despite his misgivings he did a scale drawing and then told Roberts, "I'll build one of the hands. If I can build the hand, I can do it." Lee had done some drawing in high school, and some metal sculpting. He began to construct the hand from exhaust pipes used for heavy trucks. Once he completed the hand, he realized that he could finish the rest.

Ron Hughes, one of the many non-Catholics who worked on the project, originally became involved because he wanted more experience as a welder. In working on the superstructure of the statue, he spent more time welding than many welders spend in a lifetime. The superstructure for the statue is six tiers of various-sized pipe. For months, the young Anaconda worker volunteered hours each day to work on the statue. The statue was fabricated and assembled in the yard at Roberts Rocky Mountain Equipment, the company Joe Roberts owns and operates.

Just as the birth at Bethlehem would have had no extraordinary meaning without the cross of Golgatha, so nothing good and lasting is ever created without pain as well as sacrifice. The workers for the Lady of the Mountains suffered their share of pain and hurt feelings. Primarily through misunderstandings rather than true malice, unpleasant repercussions occurred. Although most approved of the project, some even going so far as to declare the project a visionary one, others criticized, and some harassed. Crank phone calls, rude letters to the papers, and other criticisms hurt those involved in the project. Partially, this stemmed from inaccurate reporting on the costs involved. Nevertheless, even through a stormy period of controversy, the project quietly continued.

At long last, the statue was completed and ready to be airlifted to her perch atop the Continental Divide, east of Butte. No private helicopter was large enough or powerful enough to carry out the project, so help was requested from the Defense Department. Senator John Melcher of Montana and Senator Barry Goldwater, chairman of the Senate Armed Services Committee, requested permission for use of a special helicopter, and Defense Secretary Caspar Weinberger okayed the project. Among the conditions imposed was that the foundation reimburse the Army for all costs incurred in moving the statue.

Friday, December 20, 1985, Our Lady of the Rockies was completed as a giant Skycrane helicopter, flown by pilots from the Nevada Army National Guard, set the top portion on the body of the statue. Fluttering from the head were a Christmas tree, and the flags of the United States and Montana. These are traditionally used by ironworkers when they "top off," or finish a job. While hanging from the helicopter, the head of the statue turned in the wind, prompting a radio announcer to remark, "She turned around and smiled at the people." Thousands watched as the Lady was airlifted to her mountain. Ironworkers on the mountain completed the securing of the statue amid the sound of church bells, car horns, fire sirens, and other sounds of celebration heralding the end of the week-long airlift and the five-year project completion. A party that night included the more than twenty workers on the project, local people, and the Nevada National Guardsmen as well as Montana National Guard crews from Butte and Helena units that flew a support unit during the technically perilous and difficult airlift.

At the party, Mark Staples, an attorney from Conrad, sang and played his song "Our Lady of the Rockies." The words of this song are really a prayer set to music. A prayer for unity — "Make us all one family. Give us one voice to sing." The chorus petitions: "Bless us, Our Lady of the Rockies, and this land, those peaks divine. May our hearts be like your arms, full of love and open wide."

Our Lady of the Rockies, symbol of universal motherhood, grant that we may always remember those blessings with which we in America are so abundantly favored. Keep our hearts full of love for, and open wide to, others.

Our Lady of the Rosary
of the Philippines:
La Naval of Manila

OF ALL THE famous Marian images in the Philippines, *La Naval* stands alone as a "native virgin." Although her clothes mark her readily as a product of the seventeenth-century Spanish "Golden Age," her oriental features reflect the uniqueness of her position as a truly indigenous queen of the Philippines.

In 1593, on the death of his father, the Spanish Governor-General Luís Perez Dasmarinas commissioned Captain Hernando de los Rios Coronel to have a Marian statue sculpted. He wished to give a religious imprint to his regime in the Philippines. A non-Catholic Chinese sculptor was found to make the statue. This sculptor later became a convert through the intercession of the Virgin.

The beautiful image was presented to the Manila Dominicans and enshrined in the old Santo Domingo Church by the Pasig River. The image is about four feet, eight inches tall and is made of hardwood, with ivory face and hands. Over three centuries have mellowed the ivory to a delicate brown. The Oriental-Filipina face is almond-shaped, with high-set cheekbones and slanting eyes. The image is dressed as a royal lady of the palace of King Philip of Spain. On her left arm, she holds her beloved Holy Child Jesus. With her right arm, she holds a royal scepter and staff and her rosary beads. The statue is covered with jewels, tributes from her throngs of devotees through the ages. Each jewel has its own story. The halo is surrounded by twenty-four stars, and she wears a queenly crown.

In 1571, the armada of the cross under John of Austria, brother of King Philip II, met and defeated the naval armies of the Crescent under Sultan Selim II ("the Sot") off the gulf of Lepanto between Italy and Greece. St. Pius V, the great Dominican Pope, ordered the public praying of the Rosary throughout Christendom in support of the Christian navies seeking to stop the onslaught of Islam. Although aged and ill, the Pope himself led, on foot, a rosary procession through Rome. After the victory for the Christian forces, the Church was quick to acknowledge the help of Our Lady and instituted October 7 as the Feast of the Queen of the Most Holy Rosary, a feast around which naval traditions have gravitated through the centuries. From this, the name "*La Naval*" came to be known as a special title for Our Lady, helper of Christian Navies.

In the Philippines of 1646, there were not only hostile Muslims in the South, but also Dutch and English privateers who wanted the riches of the archipelago; they also wanted to replace Catholicism with Dutch Protestant Calvinism. During this year, there were five bloody naval battles between the greatly outnumbered Spanish-Catholic-Philippine forces and the Dutch marauders. Only fifteen of the defenders of Manila were lost in all of the battles. The Dutch, then political enemies of the Spanish, retreated and never again threatened to destroy the integrity of the islands by annexing them to the Dutch East Indies.

Before each of the battles, the intercession of Our Lady

OUR LADY OF THE ROSARY OF THE PHILIPPINES or *"La Naval" (photo from Shrine Archives) has a distinctly Asian look*

was fervently sought. Crew members — Spanish soldiers, Religious, and Filipinos — vowed special homage to Our Lady for a victorious battle. True to their Latin heritage and Catholic pride, the victorious defenders petitioned official Church recognition and declaration of the naval victories of 1646 as miracles worked by the Mother of God. The Ecclesiastical Council in Cavite, with the help of doctors of theology, canonical experts, and prominent religious, deliberated and examined written and oral testimonies from all eye-witnesses. Finally, on April 9, 1662, the Council ordered that the five naval victories of 1646 be declared miraculous, "granted by the Sovereign Lord through the intercession of the Most Holy Virgin and devotion to her Rosary, that the miracles be celebrated, preached and held in festivities and to be recounted among the miracles wrought by the Lady of the Rosary for the greater devotion of the faithful to Our Most Blessed Virgin Mary and Her Holy Rosary." This decree was signed by all eight members of the Church Council.

As ordered, these miracles have been preached and celebrated in solemn festivities for over three centuries. Through the centuries, there have been a number of political upheavals in the Catholic Philippines. Still the people have retained the tradition of celebration of *La Naval de Manila*.

After the 1896 Revolution, the large processions in her honor were toned down but never suspended. In 1906, *La Naval* was crowned canonically by Rome's Apostolic Legate. In 1941, her shrine in the Old Santo Dominican Church in Manila was bombed. *La Naval* was safely hidden for a time in the old church's vault, and later transferred to the chapel of the University of Santo Tomás. Here, thousands of her devotees flocked to honor her in her third centennial in 1946. In 1952, the cornerstone was laid for a new shrine at the Santo Domingo Church in Quezon City. In 1954, in a boat-shaped carriage, *La Naval* was led in solemn procession to her new home by the Philippines hierarchy, public officials, priests, nuns, and thousands of devotees. This shrine was declared by the Philippine bishops as the national shrine of the Queen of the Holy Rosary of the Philippines.

During her feast in October of 1973, *La Naval* was acknowledged as the patroness of the capital city of the Philippines. In 1974, she was enshrined in a safer vault-altar because of recent sacrilegious robberies of churches and sacred images in the area.

In 1985, a year-long celebration was held in the Philippines for the Marian year. Shortly thereafter, in February of 1986, Cardinal Jaime Sin, archbishop of Manila, called for "people power" in a pastoral act designed to avoid bloodshed over the Marcos regime's repression. The phenomenon surfaced, and people armed only with the weapons of love — rosaries, icons of Jesus and Mary, flowers, and food — were able to stop tanks and troops in battle gear. Rosary vigils and nightly processions of a replica of the antique image of *La Naval* were led by the Filipino Dominicans outside the gates of the presidential palace. Many Filipinos attribute the victory in the peaceful revolution to divine intervention.

Two of the most prominent Church leaders in the Philippines, Cardinal Sin and Cardinal Ricardo Vidal, archbishop of Cebu, have said they see the Church's role in the Philippines in traditional terms of nonviolence and prevention of bloodshed. They encourage their people to work together for peace. The Dominicans and the devotees of *La Naval* implore their special patroness here to bring them this fervently sought-for peace.

101

La Naval de Manila, *Queen of the Most Holy Rosary of the Philippines, Mirror of Justice, help us to pray for the greatest victory, the victory of your Son's Peace in the Philippines and the entire world. We ask you to help us remember that one of your most blessed titles is Queen of Peace.*

Our Lady of San Juan de los Lagos

MANY AMERICAN Catholics are familiar with the pilgrim statue of Our Lady of Fátima which travels to churches across the United States in order that the faithful may be reminded of her and of the requests she made in the apparitions in Portugal. Less familiar is another little pilgrim statue of Our Lady who also travels to visit her clients — The Virgin of San Juan de los Lagos.

The devotion to Our Lady under this title dates back to the beginning of the seventeenth century. Fray Antonio of Segovia, a Spanish Franciscan missionary, took a small statue of the Immaculate Conception to the town of San Juan Bautista Mezquetitlan, Mexico. (Later the name of the town was changed to San Juan de los Lagos.) Here, by 1623, many of the Nochixlecas Indians venerated her under the title of "Cichaupilli," which simply means "Lady."

Today, the miraculous little statue stands in the church dedicated to the Immaculate Conception and is known as Our Lady of Saint John of the Lakes. The statue shows Our Lady with her hands folded in prayer. She stands on a half moon and two stars. Her base is made of silver. Behind her, over her crown, are two angels holding a scroll with the inscription, "Immaculate Mother, pray for us."

The first miracle of the little statue was its self-preservation. In 1623, the statue appeared ragged, and the face was disfigured. The curate took it from the main church and put it in the sacristy. An old Indian woman, Ana Lucia, came daily to pray and to sweep and clean the church. Each morning, she found the statue back in the main church, in spite of the fact that she returned it daily to the sacristy by order of the curate.

One day in that year a troop of traveling acrobats came to the city. The family consisted of a man, his wife, and two daughters. While practicing a trick for their performance, the youngest daughter accidentally fell on some knives in the act and died. One of the Indians, noticing the grief of the parents, went and got the old Indian Ana Lucia. In compassion for the mother of the girl, Ana told the parents to pray to Our Lady, and went and got the statue from the church. When Ana Lucia laid the image of the virgin on the dead girl's breast, the young girl immediately returned to life. Her wounds healed instantly, leaving no trace or scar. The ecclesiastical authorities of the diocese conducted an official investigation and confirmed the authenticity of the miracle after examining the eleven witnesses who gave sworn testimony to what they had seen.

In appreciation, the acrobat took the statue to Guadalajara in order to have it restored. There he found a sculptor who restored it quickly and brilliantly. When the acrobat went to pay the artist, however, he was missing. No one seemed to have any knowledge of the artist — who he was or where he had gone. The mystery surrounding the restoration of the statue caused its fame to spread even more quickly. Numerous miracles have been claimed through the intercession of Mary from prayers before the little statue.

Today, the shrine of Our Lady of the Lakes is one of the favorite places of pilgrimage in Mexico. Pilgrims come from all parts of Mexico, and from those parts of the United States where those of Spanish and Mexican descent have mi-

OUR LADY OF SAN JUAN DE LOS LAGOS, borne from Spain to Mexico, was the first "traveling Virgin"

grated. The devotion to the Virgin of San Juan is a strong one. As all her devotees cannot come to her, from time to time she travels to them. Wherever she goes, she leaves behind her a new or renewed devotion to the Immaculate Conception. In a number of places in the American Southwest, churches dedicated to her have been built and replicas of the image enshrined.

Virgin of San Juan, just as you inspire devotion wherever you go, let me inspire love for you wherever I go. Grant me the grace to understand the great miracle in my life — that through Christ's redemption I am free.

Our Lady of Schoenstatt

O N OCTOBER 19, 1914, a German priest, Father Joseph Kentenich, and the members of the Marian Sodality under his care made a covenant of love with the Blessed Mother. Father Kentenich wanted to work toward transforming the little Chapel of St. Michael into a Marian place of grace through the conscious cooperation of human instruments. He and the boys of the sodality, with their genuine striving for holiness, would prevail upon Our Lady "with gentle force" and draw her down to that place. Making use of every opportunity that arose — all of the little, insignificant things that go to make up everyday life — the boys began to bring their "contributions" to her little shrine so that she might work miracles of grace in men's hearts and thus renew the world.

After World War I, this sodality developed into the International Apostolic Movement of Schoenstatt. After World War II, its development spread to foreign countries and it became an international movement which has cast roots in all continents. This movement includes six secular institutes and fifteen federations and leagues. It also includes pilgrims. These four groups differ from one another in their commitment to Schoenstatt; in the degree to which they have applied the Schoenstatt asceticism, community life, Marian devotion, and apostolate to their own lives. Worldwide, the organized movement has about two hundred thousand active members, not including the pilgrims.

The Schoenstatt Movement has a special mission. It is a renewal movement in the Church, offering a place to any Catholic interested in intense spiritual striving. It is made up of people of all walks of life, all states in life, all ages and cultures. The members of the institutes bear the responsibility for the constant training of all the branches in keeping with the spirituality of the father and founder. They strive for everyday sanctity and try to serve the universal apostolate of the Church in the world today. On the eighteenth of each month, the Schoenstatt family and pilgrims on all continents celebrate covenant day. They celebrate their covenant of love with the Mother of God.

Schoenstatt was founded as a work and an instrument of God through Mary. As Mary was chosen to be the associate of Christ in His entire work of redemption, Schoenstatt members celebrate their covenant with her to bring Him to all peoples and to help establish His kingdom in this world.

A beautiful picture of Mary and her Child, Jesus, is honored in all Schoenstatt shrines throughout the world. It is a copy of an original painting done by the Italian artist Crosio toward the end of the nineteenth century. Although the original title of this picture was *"Refugium Peccatorum"* (Refuge of Sinners), it is now known as the Mother Thrice Admirable, Queen and Victress of Schoenstatt. The picture was put up in the shrine at Schoenstatt, Germany, in 1915.

In this picture of grace, Mary is revealed as the Thrice Admirable Mother. She is the Mother of God, the Mother of the Redeemer, and also our Mother. Mary's deep love unites her to her divine Child, and urges her to lead all who come to her to Him.

"The heart is the innermost center of the spiritual life of a person," wrote Pope Paul VI. The human heart is the most

OUR LADY OF SCHOENSTATT, Mother Thrice Admirable,
Queen and Victress, in the original painting by Crosio

precious of all the gifts which Mary wishes to give her Son. Mary draws us to give our hearts to Him.

Mary is also honored as queen. According to the will of the eternal Father, Mary bore the anguish and death of the cross in loyal love together with her Son. Now she shares in His kingly glory and power in a unique way. At the throne of God, she sees to building up His kingdom in our world.

As victress, Mary stands in the forefront of all the battles of God which must be fought in this world. She leads us to Christ and through Him in the Holy Spirit into the heart of the eternal Father for the glory of the Triune God.

Schoenstatt's covenant of love with Mary is a means to realize one's baptismal covenant with the Triune God. Its message and great gift for our Church and time is the original covenant of love which has grown out of a living, practical faith in divine providence, and which finds expression in a deep mission-consciousness and fruitful apostolate.

Father Kentenich wrote, "Keep your place in the heart of Our Lady. You belong there, whatever happens. There you will find peace, security, and confidence in the victory in every circumstance and in every instance. Do good where the opportunity arises, and see a kind Father-hand in everything. He guides your destiny according to His wise plan of love."

Mother Thrice Admirable, Queen and Victress of Schoenstatt, help me to live each day with a practical faith in divine Providence. Let me be calm and really listen to what God asks of me each day. Accept my heart as a gift for your divine Son, and help me keep my baptismal covenant with the Triune God.

110

Our Lady of Walsingham

"Walsingham, 'in thee is built New Nazareth,'
Where shall be held in a memorial
The great joy of my salutation.
First of my joys, their foundation and origin
Root of mankind's gracious redemption.
When Gabriel gave me this news:
To be a Mother through humility.
And God's Son conceive in virginity. . . .

"O England, you have great cause to be glad
For you are compared to the promised land, Sion.
You are called in every realm and region
The Holy Land, Our Lady's Dowry.
In you is built new Nazareth, a house
To the honor of the Queen of Heaven
And her most glorious salutation
When Gabriel said at Old Nazareth, Ave.
This same joy shall here be daily and forever remembered."
                        (From the Pynson Ballad, c. 1470)

THE FOCUS OF the devotion to Our Lady at Walsingham, the English national shrine, is clear. Here devotion is targeted to the great mystery of the Incarnation . . . that moment when God emptied Himself and became man, took flesh in the womb of Mary. At Walsingham, the New Nazareth, Mary asks that Christians remember the great act

111

of love when the Creator embraced His creatures. At Walsingham, too, devotion to Mary is a call to unity and to world peace. Every Thursday, a candle is lit before the statue of Our Lady as a reminder to all, residents and pilgrims alike, to pray for Christian unity. This is in keeping with the message of the reconciliation of all things in Christ which this shrine has proclaimed for over nine hundred years. Nearby are an Anglican shrine to Our Lady, a Methodist chapel, and a Greek Orthodox church. Pilgrims to the Roman Catholic shrine are encouraged to visit these in a spirit of Christian unity and love.

Before the Reformation, England was in no way less devoted to Mary than the rest of Catholic Europe. Shrines and churches dedicated to the Mother of God abounded in every part of the country. Of all of these, Walsingham was of primary importance, ranking with Rome, Jerusalem, and Compostella in importance. As with many historic European sanctuaries, large gaps in the history of Walsingham remain. Some of these, it is be hoped, will be filled through modern archaeological research. At any rate, by the time of the Reformation this Norfolk shrine was so popular that tradition tells us that many said the Milky Way itself pointed the way to Walsingham.

In the mid-fifteenth century, a tract printed by the craftsman Richard Pynson in the form of a ballad with twenty-one verses professed to give an authentic account of the miraculous foundation of Walsingham. The tract claimed to record what was then preserved in older books which, sadly, are today not extant. According to the ballad, a widow, Lady of the Manor Richeldis de Faverches, was accorded a triple vision at Walsingham in 1061. She had prayed to be allowed to honor Our Lady in some special manner. In spirit, the Blessed Virgin led her to Nazareth and

OUR LADY OF WALSINGHAM statue preserved in the
Slipper Chapel (from a color photograph by Goodliffe Neale)

showed her the little House of the Holy Family which was then preserved beneath the Basilica of the Annunciation. Mary commanded the widow to make another house like this, being careful of the measurements, to be put at Walsingham. By tradition, Our Lady gave Richeldis three reasons for this: 1) for the honor of Mary, 2) as a place where all who sought Mary could find succor, and 3) as a memorial of the great joy of the Angelic Salutation.

The widow obeyed and called carpenters to construct the replica, but a difficulty arose as to the site. Overnight, a heavy fall of dew covered the land with a white rime except for two spaces which were equal in area to the new house. The workers chose one of these dry spots near two wells, but the workmen had difficulty in affixing the house to the foundations they had laid. Richeldis spent the night in prayer, and the next morning the workmen found that the house had been lifted and set on the other space, two hundred feet away, where it remained for more than four hundred and fifty years. A chapel, a Lady chapel, and a grand priory church were built, and until their destruction in 1538 became one of the splendors of England.

Kings and paupers alike came to pay their respects to the Mother of God at Walsingham. All of the kings and queens of England between Henry III and Henry VIII came on pilgrimage. Henry VIII himself came a number of times. He removed his shoes, after confessing his sins at the Slipper Chapel, and walked the last mile barefoot. After his last visit, he had a change of mind and outlawed devotion to Our Lady of Walsingham. He gave orders for the destruction of the shrine, whereupon it was laid level with the ground and those who objected were executed. The Walsingham martyrs, sub-prior Nicholas Mileham, layman George Guisborough, and some others were executed in 1537.

In the summer of 1538, the priory was surrendered and the miraculous statue of Our Lady of Walsingham was handed over and burnt at Chelsea. There is a story that the statue which was burnt was a copy; if so, the original has not been uncovered. The statue venerated at the shrine today was carved in 1954 and crowned on the Pope's behalf by the apostolic delegate. Today's statue was modeled after the seal of Walsingham priory, a medieval seal preserved in the British Museum. It depicts Mary as a mother, crowned in the Saxon style and seated on the throne of wisdom. She is herself a throne for Christ, her Son, who is represented holding the Gospels as if to present them to the world. Mary is holding the threefold lily-scepter of virginity. Her right hand points to Christ. The Child extends His arm in a double gesture of blessing and protection of His Mother. Each part of the statue is rich in symbolism, such as the seven rings on the throne which stand for the sacraments. The crown for today's statue is used only on special occasions. It was made from gifts from all over the world. It is fashioned from eighteen-carat gold and contains one hundred sixteen precious stones, including seventy-one diamonds.

For about four centuries after the Reformation, Walsingham was forgotten. Secretly devotion lived on, but Catholics only obtained their religious freedom in 1829, and the Catholic hierarchy was only set up again in England in 1850.

Most of the pilgrims' chapels along the routes to Walsingham were destroyed. A small chapel of St. Catherine, a mile outside the village, was preserved. Miss Charlotte Boyd, an Anglican and a benefactor of religious houses, who subsequently became a Roman Catholic, found the chapel in use as a barn. The chapel, known as the Slipper Chapel, was bought and restored by Miss Boyd, and later given to the Catholic Church. Here, in 1879, the first Catho-

115

Queen of the Holy Rosary

TRADITION HOLDS that Our Lady gave the Rosary to Saint Dominic Guzman in 1206 as a form of Gospel-preaching and popular prayer. For more than seven centuries, the Rosary devotion has been one of the most popular devotional practices in the Church. Its combination of vocal and mental prayer have made it a prime tool for contemplation. Jesus is the author and source of grace; Our Lady's Rosary is the key to open the treasury of grace to us.

Although prayer beads had been popular before Dominic's time, he and his friars quickly adopted the Rosary as an excellent way to teach the mysteries of Christianity to a largely illiterate European population. In 1470, Blessed Alan de la Roche founded the first Rosary confraternity, and thereby launched the Dominican Order as the foremost missionaries of the Rosary. Through the efforts of Blessed Alan and the early Dominicans, this prayer form spread rapidly throughout Western Christendom.

The meditations on the fifteen mysteries serve as reminders of incidents in the lives of Christ and Mary. These are divided into the joyful, sorrowful, and glorious mysteries. Thirteen of the mysteries come from incidents in the New Testament. One, the Assumption of Mary into Heaven, comes from Sacred Tradition. The fifteenth, the Crowning of Mary as Queen of Heaven, is thought to be derived from images in the Book of Revelation. These meditations

QUEEN OF THE HOLY ROSARY: relief,
chapel of the Dominican Nuns of Summit, N.J.

make the Rosary a reflection on the fundamental beliefs of our Faith.

Through the years, Our Lady has reaffirmed her approval of this devotion and her pleasure in the title "Queen of the Rosary." To Blessed Alan, she made fifteen promises to those who devoutly recite her beads. She told him, ". . . immense volumes would have to be written if all the miracles of my Holy Rosary were to be recorded." Our Lady's promises are:

"1. Those who shall have served me constantly by reciting the Rosary shall receive some special grace.

"2. I promise my special protection and great graces to all who devoutly recite my Psalter.

"3. The Rosary shall be a most powerful armor against hell; it shall destroy vices, weaken sin, overthrow unbelief.

"4. It shall make virtues and good works to flourish again; it shall obtain for souls abundant mercies of God; it shall win the hearts of men from the love of the world and its vanities, and lift them to a desire of things eternal. Oh, how many souls will be sanctified by this means!

"5. The soul which has recourse to me through the Rosary shall not perish.

"6. Whoever shall have recited the Rosary devoutly, and with meditation on its mysteries, shall never be overcome by misfortunes, shall not experience the anger of God, shall not be lost by a sudden death; but if he be in sin he shall be converted; and if he be in grace, he shall persevere and be made worthy of eternal life.

"7. Truly devoted servants of my Rosary shall not die without the sacraments.

"8. It is my will that those who recite my Rosary have, in life and in death, light and the plenitude of graces; and in life and death, may participate in the merits of the saints.

"9. Every day I deliver from purgatory souls devoted to my Rosary.

"10. True servants of my Rosary shall enjoy great glory in heaven.

"11. Whatever you shall ask through the Rosary, you shall obtain.

"12. I will assist in every necessity those who propagate my Rosary.

"13. I have obtained from my Son that all members of the Confraternity of my Rosary may have in life and in death all the blessed as their associates.

"14. All who recite my Rosary are my children and the brethren of my only begotten Son Jesus Christ.

"15. Devotion to my Rosary is a great sign of pre-destination."

Our Lady told Blessed Bartolo Longo to propagate the Rosary and promised that those who would propagate this devotion would be saved. In 1884, Our Lady of Pompeii appeared at Naples to Fortuna Agrelli, who was desperately ill. She told Fortuna that the title "Queen of the Holy Rosary" was one which was particularly pleasing to her, and through her intercession Fortuna was cured of her illness. At Lourdes, Our Lady told St. Bernadette to pray many Rosaries. When Bernadette saw the beautiful lady, she instinctively took her rosary beads in her hands and knelt down. The lady made a sign of approval with her head, and took into her hands a rosary which hung on her right arm. As Bernadette prayed, Our Lady passed the beads of her rosary through her fingers, but said nothing except the Gloria at the end of each decade. At Fátima, Mary told the children to pray the Rosary often.

Popes throughout history have loved the Rosary. Not a single Pope in the last four hundred years has failed to urge devotion to the Rosary. From Sixtus IV, in 1479, to the present day, the Popes have urged the use of this devotion, and enriched its recitation with indulgences. Pope Pius XI dedicated the entire month of October to the Rosary. Pope St. Pius X said, "Of all the prayers, the Rosary is the most beautiful and the richest in graces; of all it is the one most pleasing to Mary, the Virgin Most Holy." Pope Leo XIII repeatedly recommended the Rosary as a most powerful means whereby to move God to aid us in meeting the needs of the present age. In 1883, he inserted the invocation, "Queen of the Most Holy Rosary, pray for us!" into the Litany for the universal Church. Pope John XXIII, who was particularly faithful to the daily recital of the whole Rosary, has said, "We can never sufficiently recommend the saying of the Rosary, not simply with the lips but with attention of the soul to the divine truths, with a heart filled with love and gratitude." Pope John Paul II tells us to ". . . love the simple, fruitful prayer of the Rosary."

Many of the saints, and a number of the religious orders, have praised the Rosary. St. Charles said he depended on the Rosary almost entirely for the conversion and sanctification of his diocese. Founders of most religious orders have either commanded or recommended the daily recitation of the Rosary. The Benedictines speedily adapted this devotion in their ancient cloisters. The Carmelites were happy to receive the Rosary as well as their rule from the Dominicans. The Franciscans made their rosaries out of wood, and preached this devotion as well as poverty. The Servites wore their rosaries as a badge of that servitude which is the only true liberty. Inspired by the example of their founder, the Jesuits invariably propagated the devotion. St. Francis Xavier used the touch of his chaplet as a means of healing the sick. St. Vincent de Paul instructed the members of his order to depend more on the Rosary than upon their own preaching.

Our ancestors had recourse to the Rosary as an ever-ready refuge in misfortune, and as a pledge and a proof of their Christian faith and devotion. St. Dominic used the Rosary as a weapon in his battle against the Albigensian heresy in France. In the last century, the Christian successes over the Turks at Temesvar, Romania, and at Corfu coincided with the conclusion of public devotions of the Rosary. During the penal days in Ireland, the Rosary bound the Irish Catholics together as the Church militant. When it was a felony to teach the Catholic catechism, and death for a priest to say Mass, the Irish mothers used their rosaries to tell their little ones the story of Jesus and Mary, and thus kept the Faith green in the hearts of their children. St. John Vianney, the Curé d'Ars, declared emphatically that in the nineteenth century it was the Rosary which restored religion in France. Likewise, in the dark days of persecution in Mexico in our own century, the sturdy Mexican Catholics clung faithfully to their rosaries. The martyr Miguel Pro was allowed his last request before being shot by a firing squad — he knelt and prayed his Rosary.

A special society, the Society of the Living Rosary, was founded by the Venerable Pauline Marie Jaricot in the city of Lyon, France, in 1826. She formed bands of fifteen members who each said one decade of the Rosary daily. Thus, the entire Rosary is said collectively by the members of each circle daily.

Father Timothy Ricci, O.P., instituted the Perpetual Rosary, or Mary's Guard of Honor, in 1635. The aim of this devotion is to unite the members in such a way that some devoted watchers will ever be found in prayer and praise at Our Lady's shrine, telling their beads for the conversion of sinners, the relief of the dying, and the succor of the dead. In Belgium, the Dominican nuns of the Third Order established a monastery for the express purpose of maintaining the Perpetual Rosary, so that there it became not merely the devotion of a society, but the distinctive work of a community. A number of shrines of the order are to be found in the United States. Here, the Rosary is said day and night by members of the community. Rosary processions are held, and pilgrims come to sing again and again the praises of their heavenly Queen.

Beloved Queen of the Rosary, I thank you for your great gift of your psalter. As the beads slip through my fingers, may my heart and my lips sing your praise and my brain contemplate those sacred mysteries of my holy Faith. May my meditations on your beloved Rosary draw me ever closer, trustingly, to you, and through you to your divine Son, my Lord and my God.

Mary, My Sister

*H*AIL, *FULL of Grace, the Lord is with you.*" Then the beautiful words of ideal submission of human will to the Divine will were spoken: "Behold the handmaid of the Lord. Let it be done to me according to your word." With this beautiful *fiat*, the redemption of mankind began, for "the Word was made flesh and dwelt among us."

Then there were the years of motherhood, when Mary tenderly cared for her Child, Jesus. There was joy, laughter, work, and rest.

The time came for Jesus' preaching to begin. Mary, the mother, continued her earthly ministrations to her divine Son.

The sword of sorrow at the crucifixion pierced Mary's heart; she saw her Son on the bloody cross, and her agony and suffering united with His in the miracle of her co-redemption.

Mary's joy in the resurrection exceeded all other joys.

After the crucifixion, Mary retreated with the disciples and with the holy women to the Cenacle. Here she waited for the coming of the Holy Spirit.

Today, Mary continues her motherhood, caring for all mankind. Just as she waited in eager anticipation with the disciples, she keeps mankind company in their wait for the final days. As such, she is our sister.

Mary, our sister, stands and waits in company with all

MARY MY SISTER (O.L. of Sorrows, original drawing by the nuns), Monastery of Our Lady of the Rosary, Summit, N.J.

of the brothers and sisters of Christ. From heaven, she guides and directs her brothers and sisters in their daily living. She holds their hands when they need help. Her patience and goodness are examples to her brothers and sisters who are impatient for their promised reward. As a good sister, she encourages us to feed ourselves and the spiritually hungry so that we can witness the risen Christ in our lives, and transform the world in which we live. She joins us together in the Christian community of faith.

Mary, my Sister, hold my hand. Join me to all the brothers and sisters in Christ, and let me never fail in love to even the least of these.

Regina Cleri

I N THE COURTYARD of St. Mary's Seminary in Houston, Texas, stands a beautiful statue of Mary. Inscribed on the base of the statue is the title "*Regina Cleri*," Queen of the Clergy. Silently and serenely, the mother watches over those of her children who are studying for the priesthood; those who will dedicate themselves to God in a way very similar to the way she herself once answered "yes."

The statue at the seminary is a copy of one which is at the graduate house of studies of the old North American College in Rome, now called the Casa Santa Maria. Bishop Wendolin Nold selected the statue for the seminary as he remembered the one in Rome from his own student days there. Who first gave the title *Regina Cleri* to Our Lady is a name lost in history. The reason behind it, however, is as modern as today. Mary is truly Queen of the Clergy in a special way.

The title of Queen is given to Mary by Christian Tradition from the beginning of the fourth century as an indication of her preeminence and power. To attribute this title to her had become a common and acceptable practice within the Church. In 1954, Pope Pius XII instituted the liturgical Feast of the Queenship of Mary, and issued the Encyclical "*Ad Coeli Reginam*," which concerned the royal dignity of Our Lady. Mary's queenship is one of love and service. Thus, in a special way, she is queen of those priests and dea-

REGINA CLERI in one of many aspects: Our Lady of Vocations for the St. Joseph Mission Society headquarters of the Mill Hill Fathers in Slingerlands, N.Y.

cons who dedicate their lives to the love and service of God.

The priesthood is a sharing of Christ's own priesthood. Thus, there is a unique filial adoption of priests by the Mother of Christ. In her humanity, Mary consented of her own free will to the miracle of the Incarnation and her part in the great design of redemption. Thus the priest's first profession of total obedience is a generous act of a free will, giving himself unreservedly to God and binding himself to all that this high vocation demands. Mary was filled with complete and holy abandonment to the will of God. She saw Jesus, named by the angel of the annunciation the "Son of the Most High God," treated as mortal man, tired, hungry, hunted, despised, whipped as a criminal, and dying in desolation. Mary never faltered in her faith, even when the shadows had fallen over the cross and all others had fled in terror. She, alone, preserved faith in His divinity at this time. Priests need this same kind of unflagging faith when life brings disappointment, failure, and pain. Just as Mary's obedience brought her to an abyss of sorrow, the priest often may descend into the dark night of faith and charity. The priestly life is one of noble deeds which are labors often hidden from all witnesses except the vision of God. Here, too, the priest must be like Mary, content to remain unnoticed in his *fiat*.

For the priest, Mary is not only simply a model of holiness. She is also a director of action and a consoler in time of affliction. Just as Mary cared for Jesus, the priest is custodian of the Real Presence. Just as she was mother and helper to the apostles, the priest is charged with the care of Jesus' flock. Just as Mary tended to all of Our Lord's needs during His life on earth, so she stands, in a special way, to care for the needs of her priestly sons.

Throughout history, Mary has occupied a special place

Sorrowful and Immaculate
Heart of Mary

MY MOTHER'S HEART has the right to the title of Sorrowful. I desire that it be set before her title of Immaculate because she herself has won it. The Church has recognized what I Myself did for My Mother: her Immaculate Conception. Now it is necessary, and it is my wish, that this title which is by right My Mother's should be understood and recognized. This title she earned by her identification with all My sufferings, by her sorrow, her sacrifice, her immolation on Calvary, and indeed for the salvation of mankind."

Our Lord made the above statement to a holy Franciscan Tertiary, Berthe Petit. This humble Belgian mystic (1870-1943) voluntarily offered herself as a victim for the expiation of sin, and spent a life of hidden sufferings in the world. Among the graces she received were repeated revelations from Our Lord of His desire that the whole world should be publicly dedicated to the Sorrowful and Immaculate Heart of Mary.

"When we say 'Immaculate Heart of Mary' we recall what she received from God in the first instant of her conception. When we say 'Sorrowful Heart,' we recall all that Mary has suffered and offered for us in union with her Son, from the words of holy Simeon to Calvary, and until her holy death" (Father Reginald Garrigou-Lagrange, O.P.).

The Miraculous Medal was given in 1830, and followed in 1858 by the great events of Lourdes. In 1846, the Sorrowful Virgin was manifested at La Salette. In 1871 occurred the visions of the Blessed Virgin at Pontmain. The wonderful revelations of Fátima took place in 1917. In 1933, Belgium was favored with two independent series of apparitions at Beauraing and Banneux. Although each of these heavenly manifestations differs from the others, the same theme is common to all: the urgent, poignant, beseeching appeal of Mary for prayer and penance from mankind. She begs her children for prayer, penance, and above all, love, to counteract evil. In the revelations to Berthe Petit, Our Lord tells her that recourse to Mary under the title of the Sorrowful and Immaculate Heart is succor, or help, for the world.

The devotion of the Sorrowful and Immaculate Heart of Mary, when completely understood, has a twofold effect on souls. First, their love will correspond in an ever greater measure with the love of Mary for mankind. The love Our Lady wishes to find in our hearts is a strong love like her own. This is a love that will subodinate all else to the will of God. Souls will turn to God and utter the same *"fiat"* that Our Lord and Our Lady did — "Let thy will be done." Secondly, since it is in hearts that a change must be effected, souls will give reparatory love. In response to the wishes of our Queen, souls will offer reparation to the Heart of Jesus for their own sins and for those of the world. Mary is often referred to as "Queen of Martyrs." In imitation of her under this title, anyone who suffers in conformity with Christ collaborates in the redemption of the world by Christ. This is affirmed in the Communion of Saints. Together with her, men are called to share in the great redemption, and to offer

132

SORROWFUL AND IMMACULATE HEART OF MARY:
Our Lady of Ollignies (from Franciscan Marytown Press)

themselves — as a holocaust of love — to the Triune God.

The picture most representative of Mary under the title of the Sorrowful and Immaculate Heart is somewhat mysterious in origin. It is venerated at the Convent of Ollignies, Belgium. The picture was discovered at the time of the armistice of 1918 in the cellars of the boarding school conducted by the Bernardine Nuns where Berthe Petit had been educated. After the departure of the troops, one of the nuns was tidying up and putting the convent in order. She found a piece of cardboard on which was pasted a pornographic picture. She tore off the picture to throw it in the fire, and to her great astonishment discovered that the picture was covering a very beautiful representation of Mary. This picture of Our Lady was put in a place of honor, and soon many favors were attributed to prayers made before it.

A number of things indicate that the picture is of French origin. When Berthe saw it in 1919, she recognized in it the twofold symbol of the Virgin of the Sorrowful and Immaculate Heart. The picture shows Mary holding in her left hand a lily, symbolic to her immaculate purity. The index finger of her right hand points to her Sorrowful Heart, surrounded by flames and pierced by a sword. The features resemble those of the *Pietà*, or Sorrowful Virgin, so well known in many churches. Her far-seeing gaze seems to contemplate with sadness the sins of the world — the cause of the sufferings expressed on the gentle face.

Berthe and her friends lost no time in propagating this picture as representative of the devotion to the Sorrowful and Immaculate Heart of the Virgin. Soon copies of the picture were in demand everywhere in Belgium, and the devotion had begun to spread throughout Europe and worldwide.

Since 1959, the Camaldolese Religious in La Seyne-sur-

Mer, France, where the first church dedicated to Our Lady under this title was erected, have been in charge of the devotion. Slowly, and surely, the devotion has spread worldwide. In dioceses on every continent, aided by a number of religious orders and pious associations, the title of Sorrowful and Immaculate Heart of Mary is becoming known to those who honor Mary in order to give more honor to her Son.

Sorrowful and Immaculate Heart of Mary, help me remember that like you, God gave me many graces. Recall constantly to me, however, that He also gave me a charge and a responsibility which only I could complete. Remind me that I must earn, as you did, my own place by cooperating in His divine plan. Let me never forget that one of the greatest graces and heaviest responsibilities that I have is that of free will. Help me to freely choose good over evil. Let me share in your sorrow today that I may rejoice in the kingdom to come.

Part II:

Sing a Song of Mary

ICONS, PICTURES and statues of the Blessed Virgin all have different names and unique stories regarding them. Following are several more of the titles of Our Lady, with a brief explanation of the historical significance or story behind each title.

Our Lady of Angels

FROM THE earliest days of the Church. Mary has held the title Our Lady Queen of Angels. At the Annunciation, at the Nativity, at her Assumption into heaven, and finally at her Coronation as Queen of Angels and Men, angels have been associated with Our Lady. There are a number of famous shrines dedicated to Mary under this title, including the Basilica of Santa Maria degli Angeli at Assisi, where the great St. Francis recognized his vocation; the church in Rome which was designed and executed by Michelangelo on ruins from the time of Diocletian; the shrine of St. Mary of the Angels in Engeberg, Switzerland; Notre Dame des Anges near Lurs, France; the shrine dedicated to Our Lady of Angels at Boulogne, France; the church of Our Lady of the Angels in London, England; and the Mission of Our Lady of the Angels in Los Angeles.

Our Lady of Beauraing

I N 1932, OUR LADY appeared a number of times to five Belgian children at Beauraing, about sixty miles southeast of Brussels. The children were: Gilberte Voisin, aged thirteen; Fernande Voisin, fifteen; Albert Voisin, eleven; Andrée Degeimbre, fourteen; and Gilberte Degeimbre, nine. The apparitions began on November 29 while the other children were meeting Gilberte Voisin after school at the Academy conducted by the Sisters of Christian Doctrine. The Virgin appeared walking over a nearby viaduct, and beneath the arched branch of a hawthorn tree in the convent garden. The apparitions continued through January 3, 1933. Beginning on December 6 or 7, the children were taken to the convent after each apparition and were questioned separately by doctors and others. The extensive notes taken during these questionings constitute an invaluable document.

Although the Virgin appeared numerous times, she spoke little. Her principal words, considered the great promise of Beauraing, are: "I will convert sinners."

The Lady appeared as a young woman of about nineteen or twenty. She had beautiful deep-blue eyes, and appeared smiling. Rays of light came from her head. She was dressed in a long, white, heavily pleated gown without a belt. She generally held her hands together in a prayerful attitude during most of the apparition, but parted them just before she disappeared. In the later apparitions, she carried

139

a rosary over her arm. On her chest appeared a heart of gold, surrounded by glittering rays.

The Lady had a number of requests for the children. She asked for a chapel, told the children to be good at all times, and asked the children to pray always and to sacrifice themselves.

All five of the children who witnessed the apparitions grew up and married, and Albert Voisin spent many years as a lay teacher in mission schools of the Belgian Congo (now Zaire) in Africa.

In 1935, the diocese appointed an episcopal commission to investigate the events. Public devotions to Our Lady of Beauraing were authorized in 1943. In 1949, the bishop wrote to the clergy of his diocese: "We are able in all serenity and prudence to affirm that the Queen of Heaven appeared to the children of Beauraing during the winter of 1932-33 especially to show us in her maternal heart the anxious appeal for prayer and the promise of her powerful mediation for the conversion of sinners."

Our Lady of the Most Blessed Sacrament

IN 1851, St. Peter Julian Eymard received extraordinary favors at the shrine of Notre Dame de Fourvière in Lyon, France. Our Lady made him realize how little-known and faintly loved was her Son in the Blessed Sacrament. Devotion to Our Lady under the title of the Most Blessed Sacrament has been propagated and spread by St. Peter Julian and the Blessed Sacrament Fathers.

*OUR LADY OF
THE MOST BLESSED
SACRAMENT
(Eymard League,
Blessed Sacrament
Fathers)*

OUR LADY OF THE CENACLE (Maria d'Aglino)

Our Lady in the Cenacle

THE CENACLE was the room chosen by Jesus for the Last Supper. It was to this room that the apostles and Mary came after the Crucifixion to await the coming of the Holy Spirit at Pentecost. This may be considered the first "retreat" in the Christian Church. Pictures of Our Lady in the Cenacle generally portray her with upraised hands, praying for the coming of the Holy Spirit.

Chartres:

'Our Lady Underground'

T HE CATHEDRAL at Chartres is dedicated to Our
Lady, and it was built to enshrine no less than three famous shrines of Mary in a single church. Of these, that of
Our Lady Underground (*Notre Dame de Sous-Terre*) claims
to be the oldest shrine of Our Lady in the world, having had
an origin in pre-Christian, Druidic times. Chartres was the
center of Druidic worship in Gaul, and in a grotto on the
hill where the cathedral stands today there was an altar
erected to the *Virgo Paritura*, or the Virgin Who Would
Conceive, to whom the local king and his people had dedicated themselves. Thus, when Sts. Polentianus and Savi-
nianus reached Chartres with the Gospel, they found a
shrine already built to the Mother of the God who had yet
to be born as a man upon earth at its founding, and a people
prepared to accept their message.

Our Lady of China

PRIOR to 1949, there were three million Catholics among China's population of one billion. No exact figures are available on the number of Chinese Catholics today, but in recent times the churches have begun to be reopened, and the Church in China does exist today.

There are a number of popular titles for Mary in China, including Our Mother of Mercy, Holy Mother of Tonglu, Queen of Peace, Help of Christians, and Our Lady of China.

A common representation of Our Lady of China shows her seated on a throne-like chair, dressed in richly ornate robes. In her right hand she holds a scepter. The Christ Child stands to her left, and her left arm is protectively about His waist. The Child is depicted with a symbol of the Holy Spirit on His chest. Both the Virgin and the Child are crowned. The mother has her eyes modestly cast down, while the Child looks straight ahead and extends His arms to the world. Our Lady of China is implored to be the mother of all Christians, and to help them display their faith. She is also begged to be the mother of unbelievers, and to deliver them from darkness and lead them into the light of faith.

Our Lady of Grace

DEVOTION TO Our Lady under this title is an aux-iliary Carmelite devotion stemming from the mirac-ulous events associated with a picture of the Madonna found in 1610 by Venerable Dominic of Jesus and Mary, a Spanish Discalced Carmelite and the fifth superior-general of the order. In 1610, Venerable Dominic bought an old, di-lapidated building to convert into a convent. On a rubbish heap he found a bust painting of Our Lady with the painted image in bad condition. He cleaned and repaired it, and be-gan to venerate it. Legend has it that one night, as he prayed before the picture, the face became animated and Our Lady spoke to Dominic. She promised to answer favors, and espe-cially to hearken to prayers for those in purgatory.

The portrait shows the Madonna wearing a full veil, a blue mantle decorated on the right shoulder with a rosette-backed star, and a red gown. A jeweled crown and a necklace were added later. The head is slightly inclined to the left, and the image is sometimes called "Our Lady of the Bowed Head."

A number of miracles were associated with the picture. The painting was moved several times and finally enshrined in the Carmelite church in the District of Dobling in Vienna. In 1931, on the occasion of the three-hundredth anniversary of its initial appearance in Vienna, the revered picture was given a papal crown, presented by a legate of Pope Pius XI.

*Left: OUR LADY
OF CHINA
Below: OUR LADY
OF HOPE (rose
window at Our Lady
of Hope Center
(Oblates of Mary
Immaculate),
Newburgh, N.Y.*

Our Lady of Hope

DEVOTION TO Our Lady of Hope is an ancient Marian devotion. One of the first shrines bearing that title was erected at Mezières in the year 930.

On January 17, 1871, Our Lady of Hope appeared in the French village of Pontmain. Here she revealed herself as the "Madonna of the Crucifix" and gave the world a message of hope through prayer and the cross.

In the apparition, Mary was dressed in a blue robe seeded with golden stars. She was wearing blue slippers, at the center of which were golden ribbons forming a knot-like rosette. Her hair and ears were hidden by a black veil. On her head she wore a golden crown with a red line about the middle.

The apparition was seen by six children, Eugene and Joseph Barbedette, Françoise Richer, Jeanne-Marie Lebosse, Eugène Friteau, and Augustin Boitin. The children ranged in age from twenty-five months to twelve years. About sixty adults gathered, but were unable to see anything, although the demeanor of the children made it plain that they did, indeed, see something. The adults joined in prayers and hymns. During the several phases of the apparition, writing appeared which the four oldest children spelled out to the adults. The first sentence was "But pray, my children." Then writing appeared which spelled out "God will hear you in a short time." Next the invisible hand spelled out,

"My Son permits Himself to be moved." At the next phase of the apparition, the beautiful Lady appeared sad and recollected, and a large, bloody cross with the words "Jesus Christ" appeared in front of her. She took it in her hands and seemed to pass it to the children. The red crucifix disappeared, and two small white crosses appeared on each of her shoulders. Again, the Lady lowered her hands and smiled at the children. Then she disappeared. The apparition had lasted about three and a half hours.

The bishop of Laval, in a mandate dated February 2, 1875, stated that the apparition was a true one. Begun in 1872, a splendid church now stands at Pontmain. It was consecrated on October 15, 1900, and was raised to the rank of a minor basilica by St. Pius X. In the care of the Oblates of Mary Immaculate, the basilica is one of the great French pilgrimage places, noted for its miracles of grace.

Our Lady of Knock

ON AUGUST 21, 1879, Our Lady in company with St. Joseph and St. John the Evangelist appeared in a single apparition to about eighteen people at Cnoc Mhuire, County Mayo, Ireland. Ages of the witnesses ranged from six to seventy-five years. The three saints appeared in a tableau in front of the poor parish church. The lighted area near the gable of the church was seen by all who were in the area.

The three figures were clothed in dazzling white. Our Lady's robe was covered by a large white cloak that fastened at the throat. On her head was a brilliant crown surmounted with glittering crosses. At the spot where the crown fit the brow, there was a beautiful rose. Her gaze was fixed on heaven, and she appeared to be praying. St. Joseph stood to Our Lady's right; St. John stood at an angle to the left. At the rear of the three figures was an altar with a large cross, in front of which stood a young lamb.

This apparition of Mary is sometimes known as Our Lady of Silence, as none of the figures in the tableau spoke. The scene lasted for a little over an hour and a half.

Within two months of the happening at the Cnoc Mhuire church, a commission was set up to study the apparition.

Evidence was obtained from fourteen witnesses, and their testimony was later found to be "trustworthy and sat-

OUR LADY OF KNOCK: statuary and new church at shrine

isfactory" by the priests deputed to examine them on behalf of the Church.

The shrine of Our Lady at Knock received a special blessing for its centennial in 1979, when Pope John Paul II visited the site along with half a million pilgrims.

Our Lady of Lourdes

BETWEEN FEBRUARY 11 and July 16, 1864, Our Lady appeared eighteen times to a fourteen-year-old girl, Bernadette Soubirous, at the grotto of Massabielle, near Lourdes, France. She was dressed in white, and her head and shoulders were covered with a white veil which fell to the full length of her robe. She wore a plain blue sash about her waist. On each of her feet there was a golden rose, and over her right arm she carried a white rosary with a cross and chain of gold.

During her apparitions, Our Lady appealed for penance and prayers for sinners. At the time of the ninth apparition, the Lady commanded Bernadette to "drink from the fountain, and bathe in it." Bernadette was puzzled, as there had never been a spring at the grotto before, but she scraped the gravel away from the ground where she knelt and a heretofore hidden spring began to flow which still provides water for the healing baths at the shrine at Lourdes today. At her last appearance, on being asked by Bernadette who she was, the apparition gave her name, saying, "I am the Immaculate Conception."

*OUR LADY OF LOURDES: Grotto statue is dwarfed
by abandoned crutches and votive offerings at shrine*

*OUR LADY OF PROVIDENCE, Queen of the Home,
also considered patroness of Puerto Rico (painting from
Sisters of Providence, St. Mary's of the Woods, Ind.)*

Mother of Mercy

ON MARCH 18 and April 8, 1536, Our Lady appeared to a humble laborer, Antonio Botta, near a little mountain stream on the hillside near Savona, Italy. In the first apparition, she encouraged him to give her message to the people. She told him to tell the people to pray and do penance to avert chastisements from heaven. During the second apparition, Mary repeated three times the consoling words "I want mercy and not justice."

A small chapel was erected on the site of the apparitions, and in less than four years it was transferred into a shrine. The shrine is, today, a basilica. In the inner chapel, a white marble image of Our Lady of Mercy was placed on the rock of the apparitions. The waters of the small mountain stream, the Letimbro, which were blessed by Mary, still flow at the feet of her white image, and they have manifested the miraculous powers of God's healing, as have the waters at Lourdes. In May 1815, the image of Our Mother of Mercy was crowned by Pope Pius VII.

Our Lady of Providence:
'Queen of the Home'

T HE ORIGINAL picture of Our Lady of Providence was painted about the year 1580 by Scipione Pulzoni, a native of Gaeto, Italy. In 1664, this painting was placed in the Church of San Carlo ai Catinari in Rome. The picture was given into the keeping of the Barnabite Fathers. It was enshrined in a monastery corridor and given the title "Mater Divinae Providentiae." Many people who visited the shrine reported remarkable favors received through the intercession of Our Lady of Providence.

A confraternity under the title of "Our Lady of Providence" was established in 1774 by Pope Benedict. This devotion was brought to St. Mary-of-the-Woods College, Indiana, in 1925, and the Barnabite Fathers designated that women's school as the United States headquarters for the archconfraternity.

Under the title Our Lady of Providence, Mary is honored as the patron of Puerto Rico.

To honor God's Providence is to live in faith and hope, and here Mary is the model par excellence.

OUR LADY OF THE RIVERS on a causeway at the juncture of the Illinois, Missouri and Mississippi Rivers

Our Lady of the Rivers

DURING THE torrential rain and floods which whipped across Kansas, Oklahoma and Missouri in early July, 1951, forty-one were killed and thousands were left homeless. Property damage was estimated in excess of one billion dollars. Father Edward Schlattmann, pastor of St. Francis Church in Portage des Sioux, in the area just north of St. Louis where the Missouri and the Illinois rivers join the Mississippi, called on the Legion of Mary in his parish of 135 families to pray to Mary to spare their town. For the first time, Mary's aid was sought under the title "Our Lady of the Rivers." The community was spared, and the decision was made to build a shrine to Mary as a memorial.

Not only Catholics but people of all faiths opened their hearts and pockets to contribute to the memorial fund. A submerged street in the widened Mississippi was chosen as the underwater base for the monument and for the five-hundred-fifty-foot causeway leading to it from the Portage shore. A design was chosen. Finding a suitable material was difficult, but finally a special plastic resin created by Monsanto was selected. In the spring of 1957 the thirty-foot-high statue of Our Lady of the Rivers was placed on its pedestal, and since then the gleaming white image of Our Lady, illuminated at night, has guided and inspired boatmen who ply the great central waterway of mid-America. The statue's shining halo is a night beacon for pilots.

Our Lady of Roses
(Bayside Movement)

MRS. VERONICA Leuken of Bayside, New York, has claimed to have received apparitions, messages, and instructions from Our Lady as well as other heavenly visions since June of 1968. Since June of 1970, followers of Mrs. Leuken have held Rosary vigils. Currently, the vigils are held at the old World's Fair grounds in Flushing Park, Long Island, New York.

In a letter dated November 4, 1986, addressed to the faithful of his diocese and to all of the bishops of the United States, Bishop Francis J. Mugavero of the Diocese of Brooklyn stated the official position of the diocese regarding the alleged apparitions.

The official position is that the apparitions "completely lack authenticity." After consultation with the Congregation for the Doctrine of the Faith, the bishop issued a five-point declaration. In brief, the points are: (1) No credibility can be given to the so-called "apparitions." (2) The "messages" and other related propaganda contain statements which are contrary to the teachings of the Catholic Church, undermine the legitimate authority of bishops and councils, and instill doubts in the minds of the faithful. (3) Those publishing or disseminating propaganda literature are acting against the judgment of legitimate Church authority. (4)

160

Members of Christ's faithful are directed to refrain from participating in the "vigils" and from disseminating any propaganda relating to the Bayside "apparitions," and are discouraged from reading any such literature. (5) Anyone promoting the devotion in any way is contributing to the confusion which is being created in the faith of God's people and encouraging them to act against the determination made by the legitimate pastor of this particular church.

The directive of Holy Mother Church, as given through the legitimate authority of her Bishop Francis Mugavero, is clear.

Our Lady of the Snows

TRADITIONALLY, this devotion goes back to the year 352. According to legend, there was an elderly, childless noble couple in Rome. The couple was wealthy, and having no heirs, desired to use their wealth to further the work of the Church. They consulted Pope Liberius, who encouraged them to pray for guidance.

During the night of August 4, 352, the Virgin Mary appeared in their dreams and expressed a wish that a church in her honor be built in Rome on the hill covered with snow. The next day, the citizens of Rome awoke to the astonishing sight of the Esquiline Hill draped in a blanket of snow. The childless couple accepted this as Our Lady's answer to their prayers and provided funds for the construction of the church.

This church, the Basilica of St. Mary Major, has been restored and refurnished a number of times. The church is popularly known as the first Shrine of Our Lady of the Snows.

In 1941, the Oblates of Mary Immaculate introduced the devotion to Our Lady of the Snows to the American Midwest at Belleville, Illinois. An original painting of Our Lady of the Snows by J. Watson Davis of New York shows Our Lady of the Snows in the Arctic sky above some kneeling Eskimos. This became the center of a small shrine in the corner of the Oblate seminary. The shrine has since been moved

OUR LADY OF THE SNOWS at Belleville, Ill., painting by J. Watson Davis for the seminary of the Oblates of Mary Immaculate

to a place in what is now known as the National Shrine of Our Lady of the Snows.

In 1958, Navy chaplain Lt. Leon Darkowski took part in Operation Deep Freeze II. Before leaving for the Antarctic, Father Darkowski had a medal of Our Lady of the Snows struck and distributed to Catholic Seabees, who placed themselves under the protection of Our Lady at a Mass in the Quonset Naval Air Station chapel, North Kingston, R.I.

Our Lady of Sorrows

ON THE FEAST of her Assumption, August 15, 1233, Our Lady appeared to seven noblemen of Florence, Italy, instructing them to establish a religious order which would preach her sorrows to the Christian world. She appeared again on Good Friday, April 15, 1240. In the second apparition, Mary presented the seven with a habit, indicated to them the rule for the order, and gave them the name "Servants of Mary." The seven holy founders of the Servites built their first monastery in Monte Senario. The Servite Order became the last of the five mendicant orders of the Catholic Church.

A number of devotions in honor of Our Sorrowful Mother grew out of the fervent preaching of the Servite friars. The *Via Matris* and a number of prayers date back to the Middle Ages.

Seven chief sorrows of Mary's life have been chosen to make up the Rosary of the Seven Dolors. The chaplet consists of seven sets of seven beads each. Between the sets are medals showing the seven sorrows. At the end are three beads and a medal of Our Lady with seven swords piercing her heart. The Rosary begins with an act of contrition, the Our Father, and seven Hail Marys in memory of Mary's tears, and it ends by repeating three times the invocation "Virgin most sorrowful, pray for us."

*OUR LADY OF SORROWS is also venerated
in Mexico as "La Virgen de los Dolores"*

Spanish statue stands in the Basilica of Our Lady of Sorrows in Granada, Spain, where she is honored as the city's patroness

THEOTOKOS: Our Lady as "God-Bearer" is usually represented by icons, the most famous of which is "Mother of Perpetual Help" at the Redemptorist church of St. Alphonsus in Rome

Theotokos: God-Bearer

T HE NAME *"THEOTOKOS"* means God-Bearer. The name comes from the Greek words *"Theos,"* meaning God, and *"Tokos,"* bearer. The Council of Ephesus (431) was called to settle a dispute concerning the teachings of the Patriarch of Constantinople, Nestorius, who held that Mary was the Mother of Christ but not the Mother of God. Over two hundred bishops attended this council and held that Tradition had always used the term *"Theotokos"* for the Blessed Virgin. In so defining Mary as Mother of God, the council reaffirmed the divinity of Christ. In the Eastern churches, *Theotokos* is the most commonly used name for Mary.

Bibliography

Alberione, Father James. *Mary, Mother and Model*. Boston: Daughters of St. Paul, 1962.

Seevers, John. *Virgin of the Poor*. St. Meinrad, Ind.: Abbey Press, 1975.

Blount, Hugh F. *Listen, Mother of God!* Ozone Park, N.Y.: The Catholic Literary Guild, 1940.

Boase, Leonard, S.J., ed. *Catholic Book of Knowledge*. Chicago, Ill.: Catholic Home Press, Inc., 1962.

Cadain, Liam. *Cnoc Muire in Picture and Story*. Galway, Ireland: O'Gorman Ltd., 1949.

Caggio, Pietro. *L'avventura cattolica*. Naples: Asienda Autonoma de Cura Soggiorno y Turismo, 1981.

Cranny, Rev. Titus, S.A. *Graymoor's Name for Mary*. Peekskill, N.Y.: Graymoor Press, 1955.

Delaney, John J. *A Woman Clothed With the Sun*. Garden City, N.Y.: Image Books, 1960.

Dirvin, Rev. Joseph I., C.M. *St. Catherine Labouré*. Rockford, Ill.: TAN Books, 1984.

Escoto, Augusto Isunza. *Historia y Tradiciones Plateros y el Santo Niño de Atocha*. Mexico: Mignon, 1980.

Fenton, Joseph Clifford, and Benard, Edmond Darville. *In Praise of Our Blessed Mother*. Washington, D.C.: The Catholic University of America Press, 1952.

Gillett, H.M. *Famous Shrines of Our Lady, Vol. I*. London: Samuel Walker Publishers Ltd., 1953.

Habig, Marian A. *The Marian Era, Vols. I & II*. Chicago, Ill.: Franciscan Herald Press, 1960.

Houselander, Caryll. *The Reed of God*. Garden City, N.Y.: Image Books, 1968.

Hume, Ruth Fox. *Our Lady Came to Fátima*. New York: Vision Books, 1957.

Jablonski, Edward. *Mary, Mother of Jesus*. Derby, Conn.: Monarch Books, 1964.

Kempf, Placidus, O.S.B. *This is Your Mother*. St. Meinrad, Ind.: Abbey Press, 1972.

Kennedy, John S. *Light on the Mountain*. New York: McMullen Books Inc., 1953.

Klauder, Francis J. *The Wonder of Mary*. Newton, N. J.: The Marian Commission of Don Bosco College, 1983.

Kovalchuk, Rev. Feodor S. *Wonder-Working Icons of the Theotokos*. Youngstown, Ohio: Catholic Publishing Co., 1985.

Lara, J. Jesús López de. *El Niño de Santa Maria de Atocha*. Fresnillo, Mexico: Santuario de Plateros, 1980.

LeBlanc, Sister Mary Francis, O. Carm. *Cause of Our Joy*. Boston, Mass.: St. Paul Editions, 1976.

Martínez, Rev. José López. *Our Lady and the Infant of Atocha*. Mexico: Shrine of the Little Infant of the Atocha, undated.

McLoughlin, William A., O.P. *The Holy Years of Mary*. Philadelphia: John C. Winston Co., 1954.

Parsch, Pius. *The Church's Year of Grace*. Collegeville, Minn.: The Liturgical Press, 1957.

Richard, Abbé M. *What Happened at Pontmain*. Washington, N.J.: Ave Maria Institute, 1971.

Rubba, John C., O.P. *Blessed Bartolo Longo*. Providence, R.I., Providence College, 1981.

Sanchez-Ventura y Pascual, F. *The Apparitions of Garabandal*. Detroit: San Miguel Publishing Co., 1967.

Santos, Sister Lucia de los. *Fátima, In Lucia's Own Words*. Fátima, Portugal: Postulation Center, 1976.

The Rosary, the Crown of Mary. New York: The Apostolate of the Rosary, 1947.

Scriptural Rosary. Chicago: The Christianica Center, 1961.

Women of the Bible. Gastonia, N.C.: Geographical Publishing Co. Inc., 1962.

The Raccolta. New York: Benzinger Bros., 1938.

Our Lady of the Roses, Mary, Help of Mothers. Lansing, Mi.: Apostles of Our Lady, Inc., 1982. (*This is the book on the apparitions denied at Bayside, Long Island, N.Y. In a note at the front of the book, the publisher submits to the Church, whatever her decision should be.*)

The Sorrowful and Immaculate Heart of Mary. Kenosha, Wisc.: Franciscan Marytown Press, 1969. (*Message of Berthe Petit, Franciscan Tertiary, translated from the French by a nun of Kylemore Abbey.*)

Nueva Basilica de Nuestra Señora. de Guadalupe. Mexico City, Mexico: a Shrine Publication, 1976.

Pamphlet materials; oral investigations; the Bible; newspaper articles, primarily from: *Our Sunday Visitor, The Montana Catholic, Texas Catholic Herald.*

Acknowledgments:
Correspondence and Assistance

Chester Makowski, instructor, St. Pius X High School, Houston, Tex.

Heather Horn, instructor, Marian Christian High School, Houston, Tex.

Annie Doskocil, librarian, Marian Christian High School, Houston, Tex.

Bruno Kongawoin, student, Houston Baptist University, Houston, Tex — translations.

Samuel Victor Ball, Houston, Tex. — technical assistance with the computer.

Joanna Margaret Ball, Riverside, California — technical assistance with the computer and office space.

Sister Mary Peters, R.C. — inspiration, files, St. Louis, Mo.

Sister Mary of the Trinity, O.P., and the Dominican nuns of the Monastery of the Infant Jesus — inspiration, leads, Lufkin, Tex.

Sister Maria Rose Korasig, O.P., and the Dominican nuns of the Monastery of Our Lady of the Rosary, Summit, N.J.

Rev. Richard Flores, Holy Name Church, Fort Worth, Tex.

Acknowledgments:
General Information

Dr. W. B. Randolph, The Methodist Conference, Houston, Tex.

Charles Kropf, Houston, Tex.

Dr. John Coffman, University of Houston, Houston, Tex.

Rev. James Gaunt, C.S.B., University of St. Thomas, Houston, Tex.

Rev. Luís Díaz Borunda, M.Sp.S., Rome, Italy.

Information on the titles:

Brother David Tejada, F.S.C., Santa Fe, N.M. — translations.

Pbro. Lic. Gustavo Guijarro M., Santuario de Plateros, Fresnillo, Zac., Mexico.

Sister Anthony Clare, S.A., Franciscan Sisters of the Atonement, Graymoor, Garrison, N.Y.

Rev. Timothy Burkauskas, superior, Shrine of Our Lady of Częstochowa, Doylestown, Pa.

Franciscan Missionary Brothers, Black Madonna Shrine and Grottos, Eureka, Mo.

Gerard E. Mayers, editor, *Soul* magazine, Washington, N.J.

Mrs. Joyce Aucain, Dallas, Tex.

Fernando von Hapsburg, Mexico City, Mexico.

Sister Virginia D'Allesandro, F.M.A., Office of the Provincial, Salesian Sisters, Haledon, N.J.

175

Rev. Normand F. Mailloux, M.S., Saint Louis, Mo.

Father Don Thomas, M.S., Friendswood, Tex.

Father Joseph Pham, Our Lady of Lavang Church, Houston, Tex.

Mr. Chuong Do, Houston, Tex.

Rev. Charles F. Shelby, C.M., Director, The Association of the Miraculous Medal, Perryville, Mo.

Shrine of the Miraculous Medal, Paris, France.

Father Eamon R. Carroll, O. Carm., theology department, Loyola University, Chicago, Ill.

Father Howard Rafferty, O. Carm., Aylesford, Darien, Ill.

Sister Miriam of Jesus, O.C.D., Carmel of Mary Regina, Eugene, Ore.

Mons. Pietro Caggiano, administrator, Pontifical Sanctuary of Pompeii, Italy.

Rev. Guglielmo Esposito, O.P., Curia Generalizia of the Dominicans, Rome, Italy.

Rev. John Rubba, O.P., Providence, R.I.

Ursuline Sisters, Shrine of Our Lady of Prompt Succor, New Orleans, La.

Mr. and Mrs. Bob O'Bill.

Most Rev. Elden F. Curtiss, D.D., Bishop of Helena, Helena, Mont.

Ms. Cathy Tilzey, Assistant Editor, *The Montana Catholic*, Helena, Mont.

Fr. Edmund Nantes, O.P., Master of Novices, Dominican Novitiate, Quezon City, Luzon, Philippines.

Sacristan of the National Shrine of the Immaculate Conception, Washington, D.C.

Msgr. Theodor de la Torre, Annunciation Church, Houston, Tex. — translations.

Rev. Armando Rodriguez, pastor, Our Lady of St. John Church, Houston, Tex.

Sister M. Hroswitha, Schoenstatt Sisters of Mary, Rockport, Texas.

Rev. Brian Ventham, S.M., archivist, The National Shrine of Our Lady, Walsingham, Norfolk, England.

Sister Maria Rose Korasig, O.P., Monastery of Our Lady of the Rosary, Summit, N.J.

Mrs. Dale Rensing, Fountain Valley, Calif.

Rev. Stephen Mandry, Houston, Tex.

Bishop Bernard Ganter, Beaumont, Tex.

Dennis Smaistrla, Saint Mary's Seminary, Houston, Tex.

Bro. Francis Mary, O.F.M. Conv. Conventual Franciscan Friars of Marytown, Libertyville, Ill.

Deborah Korzak, Our Lady of Angels Association, Niagara University, Niagara Falls, N.Y.

Mother M. Angelica, Sister Raphael, and all the nuns of Our Lady of the Angels Monastery and the Eternal Word Television Network, Irondale, Ala.

Sister Eileen Surles, R.E., archivist for the Cenacle Sisters, Chicago, Ill.

Rev. Luis Chia, Seaman's Center, Houston, Tex.

Jim Chow, Houston Community College, Houston, Tex.

Rev. Joseph Chao, Chinese Clergy and Religious Association in North America, New York, N.Y.

Sister Miriam of Jesus, O.C.D., Carmel of Mary Regina, Eugene, Ore.

P. Antonio Gonzalez-Quevado, S.J., Casa Manresa, Aibonito, Puerto Rico.

Sister Joseph Eleanor, S.P., Archconfraternity of Our Lady of Providence, St. Mary-of-the-Woods, Ind.

St. Francis Catholic Church, Portage des Sioux, Miss.

Msgr. Otto L. Garcia, Chancellor, Diocese of Brooklyn, N.Y.

Rev. Msgr. Joseph W. Ariano, Vice Chancellor for Administration, Archdiocese for the Military Services, Silver Spring, Md.

Capt. John R. McNeil, U.S.N., Office of the Chief of Chaplains, Department of the Navy, Washington, D.C.

Missionary Oblates of Mary Immaculate, National Shrine of Our Lady of the Snows, Belleville, Ill.

Rev. Anselm Walker, Houston, Tex.

Redemptorist Fathers, Marian Devotions, St. Louis, Mo.

Rev. Lou Christopulos, Annunciation Greek Orthodox Church, Houston, Tex.

Don Cassis, artist and teacher, Houston, Tex.

And thanks to all of those others who helped me in so many ways with the preparation of this book.

178